Parent, Teacher, Child

Parent, Teacher, Child

Working together in children's learning

Alex Griffiths · Dorothy Hamilton

Methuen · London and New York

First published in 1984 by
Methuen & Co. Ltd
11 New Fetter Lane,
London EC4P 4EE

Published in the USA by
Methuen & Co.
in association with Methuen, Inc.
733 Third Avenue, New York,
NY 10017

Typeset in Great Britain by
Nene Phototypesetters Ltd,
Northampton
and printed by
Richard Clay (The Chaucer Press,)
Bungay, Suffolk

British Library Cataloguing in
Publication Data

Griffiths, Alex
Parent, teacher, child
1. Reading (Elementary)
2. Parent–teacher relationships
I. Title   II. Hamilton, Dorothy
372.4   B1573

ISBN 0–416–36730–5

Library of Congress Cataloging in
Publication Data

Griffiths, Alex.
Parent, teacher, child.
Bibliography: p.
Includes index.
1. Reading – England – London –
   Case studies.
2. Home and school – England –
   London – Case studies.
3. Domestic education – England –
   London – Case studies.
I. Hamilton, Dorothy.   II. Title.
LB1050.G78   1984   649'.58
84–16482

ISBN 0–416–36730–5

Contents

Acknowledgements

So many people have helped to develop the ideas and practice of PACT that it would take many pages to name them all.

We would especially like to thank Norma Chasler, Felicity Evans, Alice Hitchin, Mai Kim Tay and Andrew Reid, who have worked for long periods with the Pitfield Project; also Bill Laar, Primary Inspector, for his help and support.

We owe a great debt to Elizabeth Doak and the staff of De Beauvoir Junior School who pioneered the first PACT scheme, and to the many other headteachers and their staffs in Hackney and elsewhere who helped generate and test the practical ideas which form the basis of this book, including Grazebrook School who allowed us to reproduce their booklet.

We would like to thank everyone who gave us support and advice, including Tony Cline, Principal Educational Psychologist, and his colleagues, and members of the ILEA inspectorate.

And a special thank you to those educational psychologists and inspectors who work in Hackney. Indeed, we thank many people who work in ILEA, though we would stress that the authors take full responsibility for the contents of this book, which do not necessarily reflect ILEA policy.

The PACT Committee deserve grateful thanks for their work in promoting PACT and for the expertise each individual brought to regular meetings. Without their energy the work could not have spread so rapidly.

And we are very grateful to those parents and educationists who read and commented at various stages on the emerging script: among them Margaret Bradshaw and Jack Gilliland of Durham University Institute of Education; Dr Francis Stevens of Leeds University; and Christopher and Pamela Walsh, who teach in Gloucestershire.

Our final and personal thanks go to Derek for his patience and support during the writing of the book, and to Kate and the children – Paul, Sarah and Rebecca – who endured, at times, some lack of full parental participation.

Foreword

In almost any discussion about their children's education most parents stress the importance of learning to read and write. Whilst there is much more to education than reading and writing, much of subsequent learning is rooted in these two related skills.

Over the past twenty years there has accumulated a wealth of research evidence emphasizing the importance of parental interest and support for their children's learning. There is also evidence, if anyone should need it, that most parents want to help their children learn to read and that many do so, with or without the knowledge or support of schools. No one therefore should be surprised that when teachers and parents support each other during the initial stages of children's learning the benefits are substantial.

This book describes a project in which parents – and sisters,

brothers and grandparents – were assisted to give regular help
with children's reading at home on a one-to-one basis. The
result was an improvement in the children's reading as a result
of the extra practice of the skill and from the increased
motivation of knowing that their parents are interested and
want them to succeed.

This description of the Parents, Teachers and Children
(PACT) Project in the Inner London Education Authority discusses with realism, insight and considerable humour, the
attitudes, preparation and organization essential to the success
of such an undertaking. I commend the book to all teachers
interested in developing the involvement of parents in pupils'
learning. The Authority is indebted to the children, parents and
teachers of Hackney for their commitment to, and confidence
in, the project.

William Stubbs
The Education Officer, ILEA

1

Introduction

Children learn first and foremost from their parents. In this respect all parents are teachers – and very effective teachers they are. Arguably, children learn more from their parents in the first five years of life than they do from their schools in the next ten. This book is about parents and teachers working together to help children with their learning; more specifically, it is about parents co-operating with teachers over their own children's reading. We have chosen the term PACT (Parents, Children and Teachers) to embody this concept.

PACT grew out of the work of the Pitfield Project, a venture set up in 1979 and financed by the Inner London Education Authority and the Inner-Cities Partnership Fund. An educational psychologist and an advisory teacher (the writers) were appointed to try to help teachers in a small group of schools in a 'disadvantaged' area in their work with children experiencing learning difficulties. In our search for ways to promote this work we stumbled, through a fortunate and almost chance encounter, on a way of helping not only children with learning difficulties, but all children.

We had, of course, been aware of the importance of the role parents played in shaping the attitudes towards learning held by the children we were trying to help. When we heard that the Centre for Urban Educational Studies (CUES)[1] was conducting a research project into Family Co-operation in the Development of Literacy, we went at once to meet the researchers. Valerie Elder, the leader of the project, and her team made a strong impression on us. They spoke with conviction and excitement of their findings in two inner-city boroughs about parents' attitudes toward their children's education. What these parents had told them seemed finally to dispel the myth of working-class apathy over children's learning. Parents from all sections of the community were already working with their children, to an extent largely unsuspected by the children's schools, in all sorts of ways designed to promote the children's educational development, and especially their reading and literacy. These parents were keen to do far more, and their main reasons for not doing more seemed to be diffidence about their own ability to help children in the right way and reticence in approaching schools and teachers to ask for professional advice.

The CUES team told us that their work had arisen directly from parental concern and criticism as expressed to the Centre: a 'grass-roots' demand from parents that there be more recognition of their right to be informed about their children's schooling and more opportunities for them to participate in it. The team also told us of the then very recent piece of research in Haringey in which Tizard, Schofield and Hewison[2] had shown that reading standards are significantly raised where parents, in co-operation with schools, help their children with reading.

We were excited by the dual discovery that parents so much want to be involved in their children's learning and are so powerful in promoting it. We realized that we were in an ideal position to help to propagate the idea of parental help: the

Pitfield Project provided us with a matrix in which to operate in schools and to be in close touch with parents, teachers and children. We searched for further evidence and talked with interested people, finally presenting a selected junior school with the evidence we had accumulated and with the suggestion that they themselves might organize co-operation with parents to benefit the children's reading. The school took up the idea; they worked hard and magnificently to produce a scheme which had 98 per cent of parents co-operating within the first two terms of the scheme's operation.

The idea has flourished and spread with the help of many other professionals. At an early stage we invited a group of people – headteachers, inspectors, teachers, parents, representatives of multi-ethnic and adult education interests, and so on – to form a working committee to advise schools and to co-ordinate the work. This committee, and the movement it serves, is known as PACT. Variations on the original scheme are now in operation in a majority of schools in the original borough and in large numbers of schools throughout London. Meanwhile, work in several other parts of the country has developed along lines similar to our own.[3, 4]

We can now say with certainty, from the evidence of both research and practice, that where parents help consistently with reading, their children gain both in reading age and in the quality and enjoyment of their reading. Not that anyone should be surprised at this, for theory and common sense alike have long pointed in this direction and indeed such involvement by parents has often been advanced as a probable explanation – perhaps the most important one – for the differences between middle-class and working-class children's attainment in school. Fortunately, the argument no longer needs to rely on theory or common sense alone. But two further facts have emerged. Both the Haringey work and our own show beyond any doubt that parent-teacher co-operation of a systematic kind can be brought about, and sustained over a considerable length of time, with children from all the 'socio-economic' groups – regardless, as they say, of colour, class or creed. And the PACT work shows that schools themselves can build on the work of researchers to initiate and sustain their own individual forms of co-operation with parents over children's learning and can establish these in such a way that they become a permanent part of a school's life.

There is no need to be afraid that this means an unmanageable invasion of schools by parents. The central feature of all the schemes is that parents hear their children reading in their own homes. What it does mean is more communication between parents and teachers than is usual in schools. Not surprisingly, this turns out to be to everyone's benefit, and especially the chidren's. This book is an attempt to make available to all teachers the knowledge and experience gained from successful co-operation with parents.

Although co-operation over reading is the specific focus of the book, its overall 'message' is intended to be much wider. Our real concern is with parental involvement in children's education in a much more general way, though not in the sense in which this is usually understood. We are all familiar with the kind of parental involvement schools often foster, in which parents are asked to take an interest in the school's general welfare and to give support to its non-academic and 'extra-curricular' ventures. But this is not the sort of involvement we are talking about. We want to see parents involved with their children's actual learning; if this is to become a part of practice in schools, then we should be careful not to approach it in too generalized a way. We need a precise starting-point, because an idea like this can easily degenerate into a piece of ideology which gets little more than lip-service paid to it. The starting-point we have chosen is reading; but in doing so we want it to be seen only as an initial focus and not as the whole picture. Our concept of parental involvement in education is well expressed by the original acronym PACT and we shall use this throughout the book to avoid the continual repetition of more cumbersome phrases.

It may be pointed out that many schools already involve parents in their children's learning, and indeed we recognize this and have no wish to underrate the excellent work that some are already doing. We would claim, though, that such work rarely goes far enough, or is carried through in a sufficiently systematic way – and in many schools is still in a rudimentary, or non-existent state. Before children start at school most parents have tried to help them by introducing them to books and talking to them about reading. But entry into school itself often marks the beginning of an apparent withdrawal by parents from the realm of their child's 'academic' learning. For their part, schools seldom foster the idea that parents may still have a serious teaching role. Increasingly the responsibility for the child's developing knowledge tends to be taken over by the teachers. Yet this seeming abdication by parents means that children, according to the evidence, are being deprived of a massive and potent source of help.

This is a time, moreover, when parents' rights in the matter of the education of their children are being recognized increasingly. Rights imply responsibilities. It is time, in our view, that such rights and responsibilities ceased to be surrendered so completely to the 'experts'. As teachers, we should embrace what is already happening – that parents are actually helping their children at home much more than has been widely recognized (see chapter 2) – and in accepting this we should not be afraid of any detrimental effect on our 'professional' position. Our professional responsibility must be to the enhancement of learning.

It may seem that we are using the words 'parent involvement' and 'parent co-operation' almost interchangeably. We are aware of this, and the usage is deliberate. As we point out in chapter 8, it is difficult to be sure what exactly it is that causes the improvement in children's reading – whether it is parents' involvement in the sense of simply hearing their children read, or the co-operation between parent and school, or both – or even neither. Common sense and our own theoretical beliefs suggest both, and this is what we wish to convey.

We would also forestall criticism of our undiluted use of the word 'parent'. It would simply be too tedious repeatedly to refer to 'parent or other close adult/careworker/older sibling/ neighbour' but we would like it understood that this is what is intended, particularly where parents are not available. Nor do we subscribe to some rosy picture of the home as a place of invariable security, warmth and close relationships. All we would say is that homes and families often do conform to this picture in many respects and that even the least emotionally stable home is probably the place in which the child's most significant relationships exist. There is a discussion of 'difficult' or unco-operative homes in the section on professional concerns (chapter 5).

It will become apparent that we refer frequently to city schools and 'working-class' families. This is by no means because we believe that what we are advocating applies more to these than to other settings or groups. On the contrary, we believe that all children need the benefit of this kind of co-operation between their teachers and their parents. Our references should not therefore be seen as evidence of any kind of bias. They arise partly because most of our experience and work is in the inner city and partly because it is of the utmost importance to demonstrate that such parent-teacher co-operation can take place even in those areas of our society that have been termed 'disadvantaged'. This has not often been believed. What we now know about parent interest and willingness to be involved in children's learning, at every 'socio-economic' level, supports the view succinctly put forward by Peter Wilby that 'the parent-tutor is the only educational development since the war that promises to come anywhere near closing the stubborn gap between working-class and middle-class children'.[5]

The book is concerned with all children of nursery and primary age, with excursions into secondary age-groups, particularly where children have difficulties with their reading. However, we do not therefore think that this is the end of the story. We are getting indications that where parents have worked with teachers from the start of their children's schooling, there continue to be ways in which they want to help – and can help – even when they are unfamiliar with syllabus material. We glance at ways in which schools are beginning to explore this area, but for the most part it is beyond the scope of this short book.

We intend this to be a practical guide, and for this reason the body of the book is taken up with the work schools are currently doing and the steps that need to be taken to start and maintain your own scheme. One of the chief requirements of such a guide is that the reader be able to find his or her way around it easily. To help you to do so we give here a brief review of the contents of each of the remaining chapters.

2 *The background* looks at the rationale underlying the work being done in schools and at some of the factors – mostly human ones – that have to be taken into consideration before a scheme can be put into practice. It notes some relevant research findings, the underlying attitudes of parents and teachers toward working together and the reasons why reading is chosen as the initial focus for co-operation.

3 *Getting started* concentrates on the nature of the various schemes themselves, pinpointing what we believe to be the essentials. This chapter provides the pivot of the book. It outlines a typical scheme, containing the elements that have proved most successful in the schools.

4 *Making a success of it: the organization* explores more thoroughly the requirements, details and pitfalls of getting your own scheme into action and making sure it works.

5 *Making a success of it: the children* discusses a variety of needs of different children, including a look at particular concerns that worry many teachers and how some of these might be resolved.

6 *Questions parents ask* is self-explanatory; the chapter tries to provide some useful answers.

7 *Examples of current practice* is a collection of personal accounts of work done in several schools, written by people who have successfully put PACT into practice.

8 *Does it work?* deals with reactions and results. What do parents, teachers and children say about working together and what improvements do they see?

9 *Some variations on the theme* reviews some of the ideas by which schools have involved parents in ways that supplement and vary their formal schemes.

10 *Ways forward* Parents are now helping in many more areas of the curriculum, and perhaps learning skills themselves need to be looked at more closely in the light of parent-teacher co-operation. Some schools feel they are reaching quite different levels of operation because of the involvement of parents. Where does this take us in planning the future?

2
The background

In the past, researchers looking into the effects of involving parents in children's school learning have been notably cautious. This may have been because they were wary of the supposed (and sometimes the actual) attitudes held by teachers, believing that teachers generally were opposed to parental involvement – perhaps on several counts. Parents might, for example, use the 'wrong' methods, or might push their children too hard; inequality among children might increase because only middle-class parents would be interested enough to co-operate; the professionalism of teachers might be dissipated, and perhaps lost altogether. In any event, the idea that parents could be useful in helping teachers to teach, though frequently hinted at, was never really popularized. It tended to remain couched in the obscure language of the research journals, occasionally producing remarkable pieces of jargon, like the one we found in which 'sub-professional personnel' (parents!) used a reinforcement system in the form of a 'motivation-activating technique' to increase single word reading responses in their children, and it was suggested that 'sub-doctoral professionals' (teachers!) might be trained in the techniques of supervision. The finding here may have been a valuable one, but we did not find it enhanced by the manner of presentation.

Gradually however, and increasingly during the 1970s, parental involvement became more acceptable as a topic for serious investigation and came to be discussed in more open forums. But it was not until the early 1980s that researchers finally published evidence so strong that it is now impossible to ignore it.

In 1980, Jenny Hewison and Jack Tizard published the results of a research project which looked at the relationship between children's home background and their success in school. In a carefully designed study,[6] they took into account a large number of factors which might have possible significance – and one of these was the influence of parental help with reading. The children studied were six and seven years old; at this age the differences in achievement between children from different social classes are already well established. Reading age was used as a measure of school achievement because this is generally accepted as the best indicator of how well a child is currently doing at school and also of how well he or she is likely to do in the future.

Hewison and Tizard found that the home background factor most strongly associated with reading attainment was whether or not parents regularly heard their children read. Not, notice, whether parents read *to* their children, but whether they assumed what has traditionally been regarded as a teaching role, by actually listening to their children reading.

The emergence of this particular factor as significantly more important than any other they had looked at was unexpected, even for the researchers themselves. The great importance of their finding was the way it clearly singled out a factor that seemed likely to be a causal one: that is, if we actually encourage parents to hear their children read, we might then expect to see the children's reading improve. This proposition may look obvious at first sight. But is it necessarily true? Perhaps the survey, as Hewison herself suggests,[7] simply picked out the children who could already read well and who therefore *wanted* to read to their parents? Further, even if it can be shown conclusively that parents, by hearing their children read, significantly raise the children's reading ability, this does not therefore mean that we can easily put the knowledge to use. It is one thing to show something to be true in its natural setting and quite another to be able intentionally to *cause* it to happen.

To deal with these fundamental questions, a further research project was carried out by Tizard, Schofield and Hewison.[2] This project is very readably described by Hewison;[7] for our purposes here we record the following.

All the children in two top infant classes in urban schools were regularly heard reading by their parents, from books sent home by the class teacher. After two years, one as top infants and one as first-year juniors, the children being heard reading at home had improved significantly more in their reading than those in a number of parallel 'control' classes. They were discovered to be reading, on average, at or above the national standard, while the control classes were markedly below it – which, as research indicates, is not unusual in city schools. It has to be recorded, too, that reading at home apparently helped children more than extra help at school. Children with reading difficulties made especially striking progress: only 6 per cent of the classes with parental involvement were found to be reading at the weakest level, according to the test used, compared with a national average of 15 per cent.

But perhaps most important of all was the fact that this project was carried out in a city borough, with all the usual social disadvantages associated with such an area – yet 95 per cent of the parents concerned co-operated for the whole two-year period, with few lapses. Even allowing for the support of research workers, this is a remarkable record. Sceptics may like to note, moreover, that money set aside to replace lost or badly damaged books never had to be used (and this care for books has been true in our own experience also).

Presented with findings like these, some teachers may ask whether there is anything so new about them after all. Surely we've known it all along – isn't it a matter of common sense? And surely many schools already do involve parents in their children's learning? The answer is that although a few schools do, the vast majority do not, common sense or no; and very few indeed really work with parents in a systematic way, to help all their children toward an equal chance of benefiting. Most schools do not seem to believe that such systematic co-operation is possible, given parents' differing attitudes and circumstances. True, parents and teachers do sometimes work together quite closely at the start of a child's school life. But they tend to become progressively distanced from each other as the child grows older, until by (say) the middle junior stage, contact may have dwindled to once or twice a year on official 'open' occasions. As we said earlier, it seems that the child's developing mind is felt to be increasingly the school's property as he or she becomes capable of more complex learning and parent-teacher communication becomes correspondingly less important.

We need to try to find out why this is so and why there has been so little collaboration up to now between home and school over children's learning. It is, after all, no use finding out that PACT works if parents, or teachers, or both, are in some way fundamentally opposed to working together. And if there is such opposition, we should understand the reasons for it if we are to make any attempt to overcome it.

But where do we begin trying to identify parent and teacher attitudes? Perhaps an obvious place to look first for professional attitudes, or at all events the 'official' ones, is in our big educational reports. Of these the most relevant in recent years would seem to be the Bullock Report[8] on children's language and reading. If, however, we are looking for support for our concept of PACT here, we shall be disappointed. The writers of the report do indeed advocate contact and co-operation between teachers and parents – but in pretty well every area *except* that of children's 'academic' learning. True, they start from the standpoint that . . . 'there is no doubt whatever of the value of parents' involvement in the early stages of reading' (7·1), but it later becomes clear that what they are really talking about is parents being 'helped to play their part in *preparing* the child for the process of learning to read' (7·5) (our italics).

Bullock's writers place their emphasis on parents being encouraged to read *to* their children, in the very earliest stages of schooling, to help with 'reading readiness'. It is perhaps unfortunate that one of their very few references to taking the parental role any further seems to suggest acute distrust of the parent on 'professional' terrain:

> It would be chilling to contemplate an image of earnest young parents holding up successions of flash-cards and waiting with growing anxiety for their child to call the 'right' response. (7·7)

We agree, it would be chilling!

Perhaps it is unfair to criticize a report which does give high priority to parent-teacher communication and to the influence of parents on their children's attitudes to reading, but which was written at a time (1975) when the idea of parental involvement in children's learning had scarcely begun to be publicly canvassed. But this report, and the fact that (as far as we can find) no serious initiatives have been taken in the direction of parent involvement by education authorities or other major educational bodies until very recently, does tell us just how far 'official' thinking has been from the idea of encouraging parents and teachers to co-operate in helping children with their learning.

So what might be called the public face of education has scarcely been daring in respect of parent involvement. Still, official attitudes are not necessarily those of ordinary teachers. In our own experience, as we have suggested, teachers lack information and direction more than willingness. What has been missing until now is the evidence to convince them of the value of co-operating with parents over children's learning. But once they are sure of this, we have found that the readiness to work with parents is there. Before teachers are so convinced, however, their attitudes have tended to be more complicated. To understand these more accurately, it is necessary to see how they interact with parent attitudes, since the two are largely interdependent. It will be useful first to see what the main attitudes of parents are, both to their children's learning and the part they themselves play in it, and to the schools in which their children are taught.

As regards parents' concern over their children's learning, surveys of all kinds over many years[9,10] should have left us in no doubt. Researchers keep telling us that they find parents strongly interested in their own children's learning, even in homes where teachers have thought the topic of education could induce only apathy. In a particularly telling survey in 1979,[1] researchers from the Centre for Urban Educational Studies talked with a large number of parents, who between them represented the social and ethnic spectrum of the inner city, including the most disadvantaged. The researchers were extremely impressed with how much these parents were already doing at home to help and encourage their children's learning. Over and over again, the parents spoke of their interest in their children's education and their wish to play a useful part in it:

'I want to know if what I'm doing at home with him is OK.'
'She pointed to the writing on a label and said "That's a T like T for Tesco, isn't it?" . . . I got her an alphabet book after that and she was very interested in it.'
'I taught him to walk and talk and now he's taking his next big step, learning to read and write. But I feel shut out.'

They wanted to do more, but often were not sure how:

'Then he said to me, "No, that's not right. My teacher doesn't do it like that." '
'My husband was helping her with her reading but I told him to stop as I think they do it differently now.'

Many of the parents said they wanted to meet their children's teachers more often, to talk about the best ways of helping their children. But:

> 'There are lots of things I'm rather worried about and I'd like to talk to the teacher, but I'm too shy to go up to the school.'
> 'I always feel the teacher disapproves of me because I go out to work.'
> 'I want to know everything that's going on, but I don't want them to think I'm a pushy mum.'
> 'I hate going into the school because everyone else knows where to go, even the children. I just feel lost.'
> 'She talks to us as if we were children.'

The researchers, struck by what they had heard and seen (they found ample evidence of ways in which parents really were helping their children and not just talking about it), went into the local schools to talk to the teachers of these parents' children. They found that the teachers were largely unaware of the efforts parents were making to help their children's learning at home. Many were surprised at the degree of interest and involvement shown in some homes so disadvantaged that it was difficult to imagine where the parents found the necessary energy and enthusiasm.

We made the same sorts of misjudgements ourselves, before we realized how much parents want to be involved in children's learning. When we held a conference for parents in an east London borough, on the issue of PACT, the hall that we thought would be too big for the purpose overflowed, with an attendance of over two hundred people. The next time, we hired a bigger hall. We have run stalls in local markets and fairs (see chapter 8 for one school's experience in greater detail), and at times felt quite overwhelmed by the numbers of parents who wanted to spend time talking and asking questions. Even on a day when the market was not particularly busy, we have had small crowds gathering – and on a busy day have given out as many as a thousand leaflets telling people about PACT. Stall-holders have always been exhausted at the end of a day. This sort of venture has sometimes provoked parents themselves into taking a hand in promoting PACT. More than once we have been rung up by a school asking for more information, since a number of its parents were wanting to know why *their* children's school wasn't providing a PACT scheme like the one down the road! When all this evidence is added to that of the tremendous parental response to PACT schemes in the schools, we cannot be left in any doubt about parents' feelings towards their children's learning. Why is it, then, that so many teachers find parents apathetic – even hostile – toward school and education, especially in the inner-city areas?

'They never come near the school.'
'They sound keen, and then nothing comes of it.'
'They only want to criticize, they don't understand what we're trying to do.'
'We held this meeting to appoint a parent-governor, and only six of them turned up.'

We have heard such comments quite often. Yet at the same time parents are saying:

'They don't want to hear our views, they don't respect our opinions about our own children.'
'I'd like to talk more, but the teachers are so busy.'
'Of course, education's changed so much since my day, I'm afraid of sounding old fashioned.'
'I don't want to seem pushy.'

Uncertainty and exasperation abound in all these comments; whether or not they have much foundation in reality, they can be deeply felt.

Why do we find these discrepancies between parents' and teachers' perceptions of each other? Obviously, the researchers who go into people's homes and talk with them about their children's schooling are getting a very different picture from that of the teachers quoted above. Presumably this is not because the researchers are talking to an altogether different breed of parent! There do seem to be marked differences in what parents say when, on the one hand, they are talking in an informal situation to people not associated with the school and, on the other, when they are talking (or *not* talking) to professionals in the schools. One reason for this seems to be the popular 'bogey' image of teachers as authority figures, with schools as places of discipline and, sometimes, punishment. This image may be easy to discount for people who become teachers themselves, but it still has a sufficient hold on many parents to prevent them from feeling really at ease as they approach the school gates.

Teachers themselves, for that matter, often admit to a certain feeling of apprehension when they have to see their own child's teacher! It is usual to experience some feeling of deference when you beard the supposed 'expert' in his or her den: how many of us are prepared to sit and argue with what the doctor says? And if that expert represents a system that exerted considerable power over you when you were a child, feelings of deference (or resentment, which comes to the same thing in keeping people apart) may be accentuated.

There is perhaps something more. If it is true, as John Holt,[11] David Hargreaves[12] and many others have claimed, that our school system is so geared that the majority of children must fail to meet its standards, then it follows that most parents must know, consciously or otherwise, that they themselves have 'failed' in the school's terms. Little wonder that many working-class parents (and many middle-class ones too, for that matter) approach their child's school feeling less than completely comfortable and find it hard to talk freely and confidently with teachers.

It looks as though a considerable effort on the part of teachers is called for, to help parents overcome these feelings of mistrust and diffidence. But even the best-intentioned efforts teachers make to meet parents too often fall through. There seem to be several reasons for this. For one thing, meetings held for parents are often run as social events, sometimes with an aim such as fund-raising, sometimes a concert or Christmas play. These functions have an important place; but in our own experience, and in that of the CUES Literacy Project and other surveys, what parents are chiefly interested in is the process of education itself. This is, after all, what their children are at school for. Parents would like to be taken more into a school's confidence about their child's progress, about what actually happens in the classrooms, what exactly is included in the school curriculum, and why. Indeed, there is a strong and growing argument that parents have a right to such information, yet it is still something that few schools offer them in any detail.

The prospect of a large meeting can in any case be rather daunting for some parents, who would prefer the chance to talk informally with their child's teachers. But they would like such a talk to be by invitation, so that there is no danger of their being construed as 'pushing' – a very common fear among parents. The timing of meetings and appointments to suit the school can also be a problem for working parents and those looking after small children. Not that we should ignore the teacher's point of view in all this. It is not always an unmixed pleasure for teachers to have to meet parents in the evening, after a hard day's work, and show the requisite charm and interest. And teachers have their own anxieties as to what parents may have to say about their work, or about the way the school is tackling some issue.

Teachers say:

'I'd like to meet parents but I never seem to have the time to get to know them.'
'There's nowhere very suitable in our school to meet.'
'After a day teaching all those children, I'm tired. I haven't got much energy left to talk to parents.'
'It's difficult to explain what I'm trying to do in class.'

One way and another, parents and teachers can find themselves separated by a gulf that many of them find hard to bridge. Yet if we look back at the typical remarks we quoted, what stands out is that there is little or no actual hostility in them, or for that matter indifference; and in fact we know from our own experience that underlying the anxieties and misunderstandings there is a great deal of potential goodwill on both sides. Given time to talk, in the right setting, parents and teachers can usually find a way to break down the barriers between them, through their common interest in individual children. Unfortunately, though, time to talk with parents does not figure noticeably in the timetables of many schools.

So parents and teachers may simply not have enough contact with each other even to think of putting into practice the ideas we are advocating. And where they do try, there can be subtle problems of attitude toward PACT itself to contend with. The worries of some teachers concerning parent involvement have already been touched on. There are still teachers who fear the erosion of 'professionalism' if their skills are shared among untrained people, or who are afraid of parents doing things the 'wrong' way and undoing their own good work. And teachers may be quite right to worry about certain parents pushing their children too hard, or otherwise putting some emotional strain on them (see chapter 5). Parents for their part, as we have seen, are just as likely to be worried about not knowing the 'correct' modern methods to use when they help their children. They would welcome advice from teachers, but are not always confident enough to ask for it.

It seems, then, that we can identify a number of real doubts and difficulties. We have seen that parents may have some mistrust and diffidence to overcome, and that schools do not necessarily always go the best way about alleviating their anxieties. Schools – and the world of education in general – have been slow to recognize the teaching potential of parents. Even where parents are welcomed as part of the school community, and perhaps work in the classrooms, it is rare to find them entrusted with anything other than strictly 'non-academic' activities. And, at the other extreme, a number of schools treat parents as though their child were simply not their concern during school hours. Parents withdraw from a situation where they can so easily feel themselves inferior partners and the myth of an exclusive teachers' expertise is perpetuated. The training and skills of teachers must not be ignored in all this, but what must be acknowledged is parents' undoubted ability to help their children to learn effectively.

We believe that there is a central need to tackle parents' fears and to demonstrate to them the importance of the part they could and should be playing: it is in the hands of teachers to do this. Where teachers approach parents believing that children's learning will actually improve if their parents help them, and believing also that parents are keen to give this help, they find them ready and willing to co-operate. Teacher attitudes toward parent involvement are already changing fast and many schools have proved themselves able to cope with the problems of time and organization necessary for such involvement.

Given that we can accept the underlying willingness to work together over children's learning, we can begin to look at concrete ways of putting this willingness to work. 'Children's learning', though, is a broad term. To provide a focus and set a task that does not seem too large and unwieldy to begin with, a more specific starting-point is needed. Any such focus should attempt to meet the needs and wishes of as many of the people involved as possible, so that there is enthusiasm and commitment. What is this starting-point to be? There may be several possible answers, but the obvious one, we think, is children's reading. Most parents see the 3 Rs as the basis of educational progress and are usually very keen for their children to get a good grounding in them. And, of the 3 Rs, reading seems a natural choice for parents to begin with – it is, after all, a way of extending spoken language, which their children acquired from them in the first place. Just as important, children themselves are almost always aware of the importance of learning to read and have a strong investment in being able to do so. As for teachers, they are invariably under pressure where children's reading is concerned. It is of central importance to most other areas of the curriculum and it is the skill most frequently tested to monitor a child's progress. Such testing also monitors the progress of a class, or of a school, so that teachers are always under scrutiny as to how effectively they are teaching children to read. Yet helping children with their reading is a time-consuming business and one for which most teachers would welcome extra help.

So reading is a common meeting-point for teachers, parents and children – all have it as a major concern and each can readily understand the concern of the others. Moreover, it is in this area that we have the backing of research findings to show that a partnership between parent and teacher really will give results.

The help that parents can provide is of a sort particularly suited to the teaching of reading. Learning to read may sometimes even be best done in the home, in what is often a one-to-one setting, without distraction from twenty-five or thirty other children. And home is a good place for settling down to look at a book together, for it is usually a place of emotional closeness and security; at the least, it is likely to be the place where the most significant emotional bonds exist. There is time to talk about what you are reading – and parents are especially well placed to relate the words and stories to the child's own personal experience and interests.

It helps, too, that current attitudes towards the teaching of reading stress reading for enjoyment and understanding. Parents can readily help children to read for meaning, searching for picture and context cues and making predictions:

'Did that make sense?'
'What will happen now?'
'How can we guess that word?'

In questions like these, common sense and good teaching coincide. They can also be fun, for parents as well as children. More than anything else, a good book is something that parents and children can enjoy together. Teachers have undoubted skills and experience that most parents do not have; parents have the advantage of emotional bonds conducive to learning that schools can never provide to quite the same extent. Thus parents' work complements that of teachers – and children receive the benefit of a partnership between what are, after all, the most important adults in their lives.

3

Getting started

Granted the willingness of parents and teachers to work together, and given their agreement on an initial focus, we need now to consider the shape that a successful parent-teacher partnership can take. The Haringey research provided an initial model, and schools have gone on to develop parent-teacher co-operation in a great variety of individual ways. From our experience of these, we maintain that there are three factors which are crucial to an effective PACT scheme. These are:

1 The meeting of parents and teachers to set up the partnership.
2 The sharing of professional knowledge with parents, and of parental understanding with teachers.
3 The establishment of reliable structures to maintain the new dialogue.

All the successful schemes that we know of incorporate these three elements, and allow each its due weight. Each needs care and consideration in terms of its practical applications and its wider implications.

In this chapter we look briefly at these elements in turn, considering the role of each in setting up a PACT reading scheme. We shall look more closely at some of the implications and practical issues in the next chapters.

Meeting parents

A school's first task is to create the right forum for opening a dialogue between parents and teachers. The first contacts your school makes with parents should be carefully considered, since parents' attitudes are bound to be influenced by the way they hear from the school about PACT. If the first letter home (see chapter 4, pages 32–3) makes them feel that the school really wants their help, because it sees this as valuable to their child's educational development, parents are usually pleased and interested, and look forward to hearing more.

Most schools launch their schemes by choosing the simplest way of getting a large number of parents together, which is to invite them to a special meeting for the purpose (see chapter 4, page 40). We know that big meetings between parents and teachers are often unsatisfactory affairs; teachers may be frustrated because so few parents turn up, or parents disappointed because the meeting does not deal with the issues they really want to know about. But where the theme is children's learning, and especially where parents know that they are being asked to help with it, there is usually a dramatic increase in attendance and in the degree of participation and enthusiasm during the meeting. Teachers often note with pleasure that the proportion of fathers in the audience is also much higher than usual.

It cannot be stressed enough that the school is entering into a partnership, and that the parents with whom this partnership is to be formed have their own opinions and feelings, which need to be taken into account in the planning. The structure, presentation and timing of the first meeting need to be carefully thought through with this in mind. The school will be setting out to give parents a sense of the proposed partnership and must ask itself how to ensure that everyone enjoys and contributes to the evening. A general question and discussion time will be needed, and an opportunity for parents to have individual and informal talks with teachers. However it is done, parents should be able to feel that their contributions are important to the final shape of the scheme.

This said, we see the school as having four main tasks during the meeting:

1 To 'sell' the idea of PACT to the parents, which is not usually at all difficult.
2 To explain, without patronizing them, how parents can help children with their reading: parents are usually glad to get advice about this, so it is possible to go into some detail.
3 To set out exactly how the scheme is to be structured, so that everybody knows how it works and how they can keep in touch.
4 To set a date for starting – preferably the next day! – and certainly not at some vague point in the future.

Large evening gatherings are not, of course, the only way of meeting parents. Many schools operate on a class or year basis equally successfully, and some schools prefer to work almost entirely with individual parents. But whatever the formula, the four areas of content set out above are likely to be essentially the same.

Advising parents on how to help

If all parents are to be involved effectively in their children's learning, teachers will need to feel sure that parents are acquainted with some of the principles of good teaching. And individual schools and teachers have their own policies, methods and practices, of course, which they will want to take into account. Teachers will find it possible to devise a set of guidelines for use by parents which they can feel perfectly confident about sharing. In our experience, though, there are one or two temptations to beware of. One is to make your advice to parents much too complex, because of anxiety about parents getting it 'wrong'. Another is to insist too rigidly on adherence to the school's guidelines. Usually parents are better teachers than they are given credit for and can tell what is right for their child at a given time. So advice should be simple at first (we do not mean over-simplified), and it should be given as what it is – advice, and not a set of diktats.

The fundamental guidelines that have been proven in practice as being helpful to parents are these:

(a) Hear your child read fairly regularly, if possible at least three times a week.
(b) Keep the reading sessions short: ten to fifteen minutes is plenty. (After all, how many children can be heard reading as regularly and for as long in school?) Five minutes of good reading experience is probably worth hours of boring struggle. And you have to consider your own time: you are less likely to be able to keep up the home reading if the demands you are making on yourself are too heavy.
(c) Praise your child as often as possible: for reading a difficult word, or self-correction of a wrong word; for reading a sentence well; for finishing a chapter; for remembering to bring the book home!
(d) Talk about the book, and show an interest in it: reading is about developing language and understanding, as well as just getting the words right. Where you can, relate the reading to your child's own experience and interests.
(e) Make sure the sessions are enjoyable. Don't have a session when you are thinking about some nagging job, or when the child's (or your own!) favourite television programme is on – you should both be comfortable and relaxed. Try not to get impatient, and if you find yourself scolding, stop the session.

(f) If your child makes a mistake, all you have to do is. . . . It is here that the policy of the individual school or teacher has most bearing. At first the advice will be straightforward; later, dialogue between teacher and parent about such techniques can become more complex, based as it will be on their common experience of an individual child. It may be useful at first to give a rule, such as 'count to five slowly and then give him the word', or 'try to get her to guess from the first letter, and if she can't, then give her the word', or 'see if he can read to the end of the sentence, and guess the word that way'.

All this advice can be given to parents at the first meeting, but it is important to present it in at least one other form as well. Most schools produce their own booklet (see figure 1, chapter 4, pages 34–9), and some have made short videos to show how, and how not, to hear children read (chapter 4, pages 33 and 40). Some ambitious teachers have even presented these themes in the form of role play.

Keeping in touch

This is the most difficult area to tackle and it is here that practical organization matters most. Unless there is regular contact between teacher and parent, there cannot be a real dialogue. PACT can be sustained only if parents and teachers regularly communicate to each other their interest in a child's progress, or lack of progress. If this is not done the feeling of partnership flags, and even where parents continue to hear their child read, the child loses the knowledge that parent and teacher are co-operating for his or her benefit.

Experience has shown that the most successful, and simple, way of maintaining contact is by means of a record card (see figure 2, chapter 4, page 42). Every time a book is sent home it is accompanied by this card. There is space for the name of the book or other reading material to be entered and for the parents to write in such things as how many pages were read and how long the reading session lasted. Most important of all, there is space for parents and teachers to make comments about how the reading is going, or anything else they want to say. Both book and card travel in a stout and readily identifiable folder, with the child's name and the address of the school on it, in case of forgetfulness on the bus.

This method gives immediate contact of an easy and informal kind. Whole conversations can take place between parents and teachers who might not recognize each other in the street! Parents' difficulties and questions can be sorted out and teachers can tap the wealth of knowledge parents have of their own children; thus the card, constructively used, sustains the dialogue and becomes a means of learning for both sides of the partnership.

Schools have found no replacement for this card as the central means of communication, but it needs to be supplemented by opportunities for direct contact as well. It is very important that parents and teachers know they can easily meet each other when they want to, and some teachers make themselves available at a regular time each week – say, for half an hour after school on a particular evening, or before school one morning. Other opportunities occur where schools hold follow-up meetings, focusing on difficulties or issues that have arisen during home reading. And letters, booklets and information sheets keep parents in touch with teachers, and up to date about what is happening in the school.

In the end, the success of any PACT scheme is bound to be dependent largely on the effort and enthusiasm the individual teacher is prepared to put into it. A teacher who takes the trouble to enter into a sensitive dialogue with parents will be well rewarded by the sense of partnership and the sharing of responsibility that results. In the next chapter, we explore practical aspects of this partnership in greater depth.

4

Making a success of it: the organization

The success of your PACT scheme will depend to a great extent on careful planning and attention to detail, and in these respects there is much to be learned from the experience of others. The topics we cover in this chapter are those which we believe call for detailed consideration, and the suggestions we make have been tried and tested in practice by many schools. The topics are:

1 The importance of reaching agreement among the staff.

2 Time commitment and teachers' workloads.

3 First approaches to parents and children.

4 A pattern for the first meeting.

5 Keeping the record cards.

Reaching agreement among the staff

Any school will find it difficult to make successful contact with parents unless its own teachers have arrived at a good measure of agreement among themselves. It is essential that, before embarking on a scheme of your own, you allow plenty of time to talk through the issues involved in PACT. Each school has to decide for itself whether it is ready to involve parents in their children's work – and if this is agreed on, there has to be a broad consensus on the best ways of doing it: 'mixed messages' to parents, whether over general PACT policy or smaller points of reading technique, are better avoided where possible.

Most important of all, though, a common agreement will help you to co-operate more easily on what will, to begin with, be a considerable task. A school does need to be well prepared for work with parents: staff need time to grasp the issues involved and to plan their own PACT scheme in some detail. You will want to ensure that the school is properly equipped with a good stock of books suitable for sending home. And you will need to share out the responsibilities involved, so that somebody – the head, the language postholder, a 'sub-committee' – agrees to take on the bulk of the planning and accepts overall responsibility for the scheme. You may want to form working parties – to compose letters, design posters and produce record cards, booklets and any other material you decide is needed. And later, when the scheme is in operation, staff will look to each other for co-operation in the dozens of small contingencies that arise during an undertaking that involves so many people. No school can hope to run a scheme like this successfully without substantial agreement and co-operative work.

The foregoing, we hasten to add, applies only where the whole school has decided to become involved. We certainly would not want to discourage an individual teacher prepared to run his or her own PACT class scheme, which we have seen done very successfully where the school as a whole was not yet ready to run a full scheme.

Time commitment and teachers' workloads

It must be increasingly, perhaps alarmingly, clear that PACT is going to demand a considerable amount of teachers' time. This commodity is scarce enough anyway, and teachers may feel daunted at first by the prospect of what looks like huge demands on their time and energy. Yet many schools have managed to solve this problem, finding ways of arranging the workloads so that in the end nobody has felt overwhelmed or over-committed. Like so many things, it is largely a question of co-operative planning.

What are the inescapable demands on teachers' time? In the first place, a number of times have to be set aside each week to go through the children's reading cards, noting the parents' comments and adding your own. These times do need to be built into your timetable on a regular basis, or the practice can slip, so are best integrated into periods when children are getting on with quiet activities. Many schools set aside half an hour each day – first thing in the morning is a good time – for reading activities, during which the teacher deals with record cards and has a word with some of the children about how their reading at home is going. This has been found to be a very useful period: rightly used, it links home and school in a personal way for each child. It can be harder for a secondary school to find quiet class times like this, but some schools have used opportunities like 'tutor times', or extended the class teacher's registration period in the mornings. In one school, the special needs department used the library at lunchtimes, with the teachers operating a rota system to see cards and talk with the children.

The other main demand on time is that needed to make teachers more available to parents. We have already suggested that a simple way of doing this is to tell parents that their child's teacher will stay at the school for, say, half an hour on a certain day each week, or come in early one morning. This is not difficult to manage for most teachers, provided they can choose the day themselves. It is an important arrangement to make, because it is their own child's teacher that parents usually want to see, not the deputy head or a liaison teacher, or someone with 'special responsibility'.

We are not suggesting that a school should turn down any extra help of this kind, of course, especially if the local authority should be generous enough to offer a liaison worker with responsibility for the PACT scheme! Help from such a source will be invaluable when it comes to co-ordinating the work, visiting homes and seeing parents over particular issues or when classroom teachers are not available. Some schools have been able to appoint such a liaison teacher, and some have allowed specific periods during the school day when teachers are freed to see parents; but these are still exceptions, and the schemes can work well without such luxuries, given a degree of commitment from teachers.

Apart from the necessary routine demands on time, there are the irregular occasions for which time must be found: for meetings to do the planning, for the first meeting with parents, for occasional further meetings and perhaps home visits. And, once the scheme is going well, schools may become more ambitious. Parents might be asked to help with other areas of the curriculum, perhaps, or a school could invite parents to evening workshops at which particular aspects of the curriculum are presented for discussion. It is certainly not unknown for changes to be made as a result of parent comments at such meetings. Undoubtedly, from this point on, the work could begin to seem endless – it is then up to each school to determine the balance between what would be ideally desirable and what is possible without risking staff breakdown!

If it seems too demanding to start with the whole school, the involvement of parents can be introduced gradually. One secondary school ran a pilot project with a small number of children and only when convinced that it was a success included the whole first year in the scheme. Along similar lines, a large junior school launched PACT for its first-year children only, repeated the exercise with the first-year children the following year, and is continuing with a gradual build-up until the whole school becomes involved. Another school found, though, that it was a mistake to start with the older juniors, who do not necessarily take to such a new practice in their final year at the school.

We accept that the demands on time and energy can be heavy. But once a school has found the time and its scheme is under way, the rewards can be weighed against the effort, and then the extra time given begins to look less like a sacrifice and more like an investment.

First approaches to parents and children

Your planning will have taken into account the day that the scheme is to start, so that the timing of letters, meetings and advance publicity is geared to this date. As we have said, the first letter home is very important in making parents feel that their contribution is something the school needs and will value. It makes an extra impact if the letter bears a slogan, logo or picture that the staff have chosen to represent the scheme, and which will be displayed on all communications, posters, booklets and so on. A bold slogan such as 'HELP US TO HELP YOUR CHILD' is very effective and constant use of catch phrases like 'Read with your child' or 'Share a good book' help to get central points across. Don't forget that the children themselves are important advocates: if the idea of reading at home has been thoroughly canvassed with them, and their enthusiasm roused, most parents are likely to have heard a good deal about it before the first letter arrives.

Talking with children beforehand is in any case essential to the scheme's success. There has sometimes been a danger of parents and teachers getting carried away by the excitement of co-operating with each other, and seeing the whole thing in terms of adult communication, forgetting to include in the planning those people for whom everything is being designed. PACT is necessarily a partnership of *three* sides. So make sure the children are well informed about the reasons for the reading scheme, how they are to play their part and how it is all to be organized. It goes without saying that the more this is done in the form of discussion in which the children participate, and the less as a set of demands and instructions, the greater the co-operation you are likely to get from this very important quarter.

The first letter to parents is likely to be an invitation to a meeting that will start the scheme, since most schools choose to begin in this way. A big meeting like this gives everyone a sense of launching the PACT scheme properly, and not just slipping into it. It suggests an effort by the whole school, saying to parents: 'We're committed: what about you?' Make sure the school is well prepared for such a meeting. You need to have discussed the ideas behind the scheme thoroughly, for at least two good reasons. One is that your presentation needs to be clear and convincing, since the idea is not likely to be a familiar one; the other is that parents' questions can sometimes put teachers on the spot if they have not thought things through (see chapter 6).

You also need to be prepared in practical ways, with attractive materials for use in the scheme. The quality of these materials has a part to play in the scheme's success or failure. A stout transparent plastic file for carrying books home, for instance, though it costs more than a card one, is nevertheless an investment. We all know that children are less likely to lose, or allow to be damaged, attractive things that look as though they deserve to be taken care of.

Ideally, when parents come to the meeting they will find colourful posters (one of them a permanent chart showing times when teachers will be available to see them during the week), well-produced 'Home reading cards' and a booklet advising 'How to hear your child read', or similar (see Figure 1). Some schools obtain children's books on a sale-or-return basis and run a bookstall at the meeting, so that parents can actually buy books to read with their children on the spot, and this is always popular.

You may also have produced your own video, starring children and teachers from the school, and demonstrating how, and how not, to hear children read. This is a great audience

READING TOGETHER

It is important that your child learns to read well.

As a parent you can help a lot.

Short friendly sessions full of praise and encouragement from you will help your child most.

Figure 1   Booklet compiled by school to assist parents reading with their children

When should you read together ?

Anytime that you can spare 10mins

How often ?

About three times a week but NOT
when a favourite T.V. programme
is on.

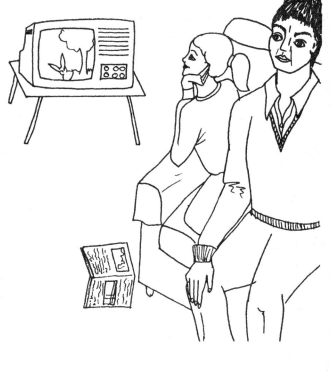

What should you read ?

We will provide books from school with a Report Card.

There is a space on the card for you to write any comments or questions you have.

Also your child can join Stoke Newington Library to borrow books without charge.

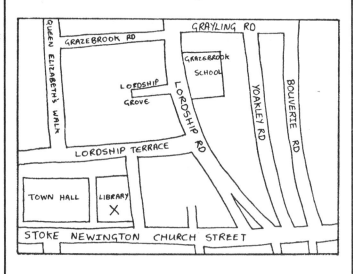

A book is a story.

Talk with your child about the story. Use the pictures. Fluent readers can talk to you about the book they are reading.

Your child should enjoy reading with you. Try not to worry him/her.

If you have any problems come and see your child's teacher. Each teacher will be there 3.30-4.00pm one evening a week to see you.

What should you do when your child gets stuck on a word ?

1) Let him/her try - perhaps guessing from the rest of the sentence.

- or guessing from looking at the pictures.
- or from the first letter of the word.

2) If that doesn't work quickly don't get cross! Just tell him/her the word and carry on.

We have a Book Club once a week
in school. Every week there is
a selection of new and second
hand books to buy.

Centerprise is the local book
shop with a good selection of
children's books. Stop off and
have a cup of coffee there on
your way to Ridley Road!

attraction: the children excite pride, the teachers are a source of mirth. The 'How not to' video can be very funny: teachers sit apart from the child and gaze into the distance, yawn, scratch their heads and look at their watches, miss the child's questions and ignore his or her errors. Or they sit and glower over the child, picking him or her up on the least detail, becoming increasingly impatient and finally losing their tempers. Even though the child making the video knows quite well what is going on, it soon becomes abundantly clear how this kind of treatment is affecting his or her reading. And no matter how obvious the caricature, there is usually enough truth in the awful teacher portrayals to give teachers and parents unpleasant twinges of recognition. Video is a useful tool for putting your messages across in a very telling way.

A pattern for the first meeting

Each school will have its own ideas about the form of the first meeting, for it will want to take into account its own preferences and skills, the age-range and abilities of the children and the school's traditions. So what we give here are only guidelines, indicating what others have found effective. Try to get a full staff turn-out at the meeting if at all possible, because you want to tell parents how important you think this partnership will be. Parent attendances are likely to be much higher than usual, so plan accordingly. Think about seating: a fairly informal, semi-circular pattern works well. Try to time the meeting early enough to get parents in before they have settled down for the evening, but late enough to include those coming in from work; it makes a big difference if one or two teachers or helpers are prepared to run a crèche, so that parents with young children can come more easily (perhaps local secondary school children could be co-opted to help with this?). Allow about one-and-a-half hours for the meeting. It is a good idea to run it in two parts, with the presentation first and a discussion later, and a break for tea in the middle. This break gives parents and teachers a chance to talk informally, which often makes for a better discussion time as well as giving parents who don't like talking in public the chance to ask questions. If you have many parents who speak other languages, consider whether an interpreter or two would be useful.

The evening starts, of course, with a warm welcome to parents for taking an interest and coming along. Usually it will be the head who introduces the meeting and gives the general presentation of the theme. Then the various other aspects can be presented by other speakers, to keep the format varied. Speakers could include the postholder responsible for the scheme; a visiting speaker from, say, the local children's library; or an adviser or inspector with an interest in the school. Brief all speakers not to go on for too long – it is surprising how much there is to say!

Within the four main themes already discussed (see chapter 3), there will be a wealth of detail dependent on the individual school's philosophy and organization. It will be important to allow some time to discuss children's books and other reading materials and what teachers hope children will get from them: encourage parents to read all sorts of things with their children, not just relying on materials sent home by the school. Reassure them also that the new scheme does not mean any lessening of reading help from teachers. Some other themes which may arise in the informal discussion time are considered in chapter 6. A good way to finish the evening is with a 'How to' video which will, one hopes, leave people with an image of good practice to think about.

Keeping the record cards

Record cards (figure 2), by their nature, do not allow much space for comment, and generally speaking this is a good thing. Too much space could seem like a tacit demand, and take all the pleasure out of keeping the card going backwards and forwards. This card is central to a PACT scheme so writing in it must not be allowed to become a chore, which would be the quickest way to its demise. Most comments are best kept brief

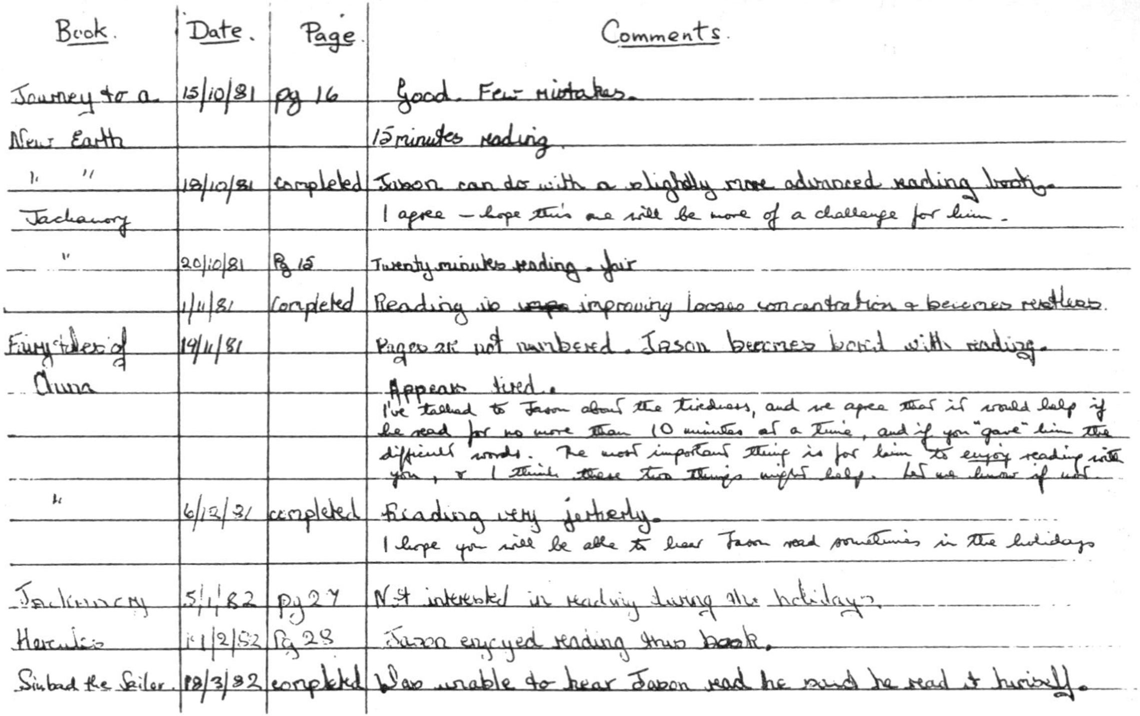

Book	Date	Page	Comments
Journey to a New Earth	15/10/81	Pg 16	Good. Few mistakes.
"	18/10/81	completed	15 minutes reading / Jason can do with a slightly more advanced reading book. I agree - hope this one will be more of a challenge for him.
Jackanory	20/10/81	Pg 16	Twenty minutes reading for...
"	4/11/81	completed	Reading is improving. Concentration a becomes restless.
Fury/leg of a Juna	19/11/81		Pages are not numbered. Jason becomes bored with reading. Appears tired. I've talked to Jason about the tiredness, and we agree that it would help if he read for no more than 10 minutes at a time. And if you gave him the difficult words. We want Jason to enjoy reading and think if we lower the expectations there will be less pressure on him.
"	6/12/81	completed	Reading very jerkily. I hope you will be able to hear Jason read sometime in the holidays.
Jackanory	5/1/82	Pg 27	Not interested in reading during the holidays?
Heroics	11/2/82	Pg 28	Jason enjoyed reading this book.
Sinbad the Sailor	19/3/82	completed	I was unable to hear Jason read he read it quickly.

Figure 2 Child's home reading card

and if something longer is necessary, it can be attached to the card as a note. There is, of course, no requirement on either parent or teacher to comment every time – quite often there will be little or nothing to say. Even commonplace or repetitive remarks, though, are worth putting down: often it is not the content of what you write, but the fact that you have taken the trouble to say something to each other that counts.

Encourage parents to comment, of course, but don't forget that some people have difficulty in committing themselves to the written word, and a few parents will be unable to write, or write in English, at all. So it should be made clear that if only the number of pages read, or the length of time spent, is recorded, that in itself is a comment, and a helpful one. Where you know that parents are able to write, but seem to need encouragement to commit themselves to paper, try asking a direct question on the card: 'I think there has been an improvement in the last two weeks – what do you think?' and let the child know what you have written, saying how interested you will be in the answer. Always, of course, tell the child what you have written where you believe the parent cannot read, or cannot read English.

Teachers' comments, where possible, should be encouraging and constructive:

'Yes, I find it difficult to get Jane to concentrate too – have you tried talking about the pictures first?/Keeping the sessions to five minutes only?/Taking turns reading a sentence or page each?'

'Glad you both enjoyed the book – would you like Daren to bring home another on the same subject?'

'Yes, I agree his reading is improving – I'm sure reading with you has a lot to do with it.'

'When she guesses a word nowadays, it almost always makes sense – that's a big improvement.'

Parents' comments can be instructive:

'She got upset reading that book you sent, it reminded her of an accident she had when she was two.'

'If you show an interest in his nan, he'll eat out of your hand.'
'Could we have a book that isn't about rabbits?'

Or may indicate where guidance could be helpful:

'We went on for an hour last night, but I think she got a bit tired.'
'I'm not sure if I ought to be pulling him up more often.'

The card may get used for other purposes:

'Sorry she was away yesterday, but she had earache.'
'She told me last night she wanted to be in the play, but she was too shy to say so.'

Before long, dialogue can take on its own character:

'We struggled last night' . . . 'I sympathize – imagine it with twenty-seven of them!' . . . 'Rather you than me!'

Some schools provide a column for children's comments, which can be illuminating – giving the child him or herself the chance to join in the dialogue actively:

'I read six new words.'
'My Nan said the book was too babyish.'
'Dad thinks I read fantastic.'

This practice is especially valuable for older children: it is important for them to be able to evaluate their progress for themselves:

'When I started reading to my Mum I didn't liked reading much. But she showed me a story she used to like when she was young and then I saw the point of it, it was a great story.' (12-year-old girl)

We have talked about finding time to write in the record cards, but there is also the question of their organization, so that you can deal with them as efficiently as possible. One solution is to have two large boxes at the door as the children come into the classroom in the morning, one labelled 'I read last night' and the other 'I didn't read'. Children drop their folders in these boxes, and the teacher need deal only with those left in the first box; the children retrieve their folders as they leave for home. Or, of course, children simply do not bring their folders in when they have not read: either way, the teacher can keep a check on the frequency of the home reading sessions. You will also find it helpful to keep a record of what is happening from day to day, with notes on such commonly occurring contingencies as 'Joanne promised to bring book tomorrow', and 'Terry asked to keep book for a week'.

When young children choose a book, it is useful to have a selection of ready-printed cards to slip into it if you want to indicate to the parent what you feel about the book's standard of difficulty for the child:

I can read this book easily.
I can read this book if you help me.
Please read this book for me.

and so on. Other useful ready-printed notes remind parents of such practical details as the return of the reading folder that has not appeared for over a week!

When they are complete, the record cards can go into the child's permanent school record, to which they provide a useful and informative addition. You will find that staff meetings are valuable from time to time to discuss the upkeep of the cards and how to develop strategies to make them increasingly useful. Some schools also write letters to parents at the end of each term and/or the beginning of a new one, thanking them for keeping the cards up during the term and encouraging them to do so in the coming term. These letters may tell the parents the school's latest thinking on how the record-card system is developing, and ask if they have any comments to make on this themselves.

The individual variations and possibilities in running a PACT scheme are endless and we have tried only to give a flavour of some of the aspects we consider important. Schools themselves must take this further, integrating the ideas into their own personal ways of meeting, setting up and maintaining dialogue with parents. Each school's dialogue will be enjoyable and useful in direct proportion to the attention it pays to the needs and wishes of the individuals participating in it.

5

Making a success of it:
the children

So far we have assumed a straightforward situation in which teachers make plans and carry them through, in co-operation with parents and children, to arrive at the happy position of a typical PACT scheme in full and successful operation. Needless to say, no real-life scenario will run quite like this. It is time to look more closely at the position of the recipients of a PACT scheme: the children. This will involve us in asking some very important questions about just how a scheme can adapt itself to a variety of different children's needs.

The well-adjusted primary school child, who is part of a supportive family which is keen to co-operate with the school, is perhaps our yardstick. Such a child does not need much extra attention from us: we can feel confident that he or she will benefit from the scheme, if any child will. We need to ask about children who do not conform to this pattern, and who may therefore need more attention to be sure that they benefit from the scheme: the very young child or the teenager; the child with special needs; the child whose parents are not emotionally well fitted to help with his or her learning, or who do not wish to co-operate with a PACT scheme. We explore these issues under the following headings:

1 Children with 'unsuitable' or 'difficult' parents.
2 Children whose parents aren't interested.
3 Children with special needs.
4 The 'under-fives' and the 'over-elevens'.

Children with 'unsuitable' or 'difficult' parents

Teachers may be concerned when instigating a PACT scheme that certain children will gain little advantage from learning with their parents and that there may even be some detrimental effects. The usual examples mentioned are parents who are very competitive; those who have negative attitudes towards their children; those who will insist on using the wrong methods; and those who are over-anxious.

Some teachers have been particularly concerned with the issue of 'competitive' parents, who are always comparing their child's progress with that of others, especially where the school has a reading scheme with readily identifiable grades. The Bullock Report expressed this worry:

> Once a child begins to read the first book of a graded series there is great temptation for the parent to think in terms of rate of progress. When this happens, parent and child begin to lose the excitement and sheer pleasure that the first contact with books should provide. These qualities are replaced by a concern for measurable endeavour, and the desire to read may become secondary to a desire to perform to please the parent by progressing through the scheme. (7.16)

Of course a school will want to colour-code or otherwise grade its books,[13] but we believe it is important that children should be able to take home a wide variety of reading material.

Even where children choose to read at home from a formal scheme, however, experience suggests that when 'competitive' parents are involved in home reading they lose some of their competitiveness. The reason appears to be that once they are fully aware of how reading is now taught (through the assumption that enjoyment leads to greater progress) they will try to work in the best interests of their child and follow the guidelines given out by the school. All competitors will go along with good practice, provided it is sufficiently explained to them why it is good practice.

This also applies to parents who are anxious and over-concerned about their child's progress or their own capacity to help. These parents may, however, need some extra help from the teacher. Whereas the so-called 'competitive' or 'pushy' parents will usually have the confidence to help their own child once they know how to do so, the anxious parent may need more support. One anxious mother we met said that her son finds her 'bossy' but sees his grandfather as kind and tolerant, and suggested that surely he would be a better person to hear the child read on a regular basis. In her case she was absolutely right, and while she heard him read occasionally, he went most of the time to his grandfather. Perhaps as he becomes a more competent reader he will put up with his mother's 'bossiness'. Needless to say, it is not helpful for teachers to try to push parents into doing something they feel they cannot do; encourage by all means, or look for other solutions, but pushing may only make a parent feel more incompetent.

Still other parents may have some form of negative attitude towards their children, but we have often found that such parents can change and their children gain from a formal PACT scheme. We know of a number of children who, for about ten minutes an evening while being heard to read, have a very different parent – a parent who is following the school's guidelines closely. Careful adherence to advice about warmth and praise can replace a parent's usual negative patterns. Some of these parents and children have developed a much better relationship, and it is the enjoyable reading session which seems to be the main cause. Terry, for example, a nine-year-old who was failing at school, was under considerable pressure from his mother who continually called him a failure – she also placed a good deal of blame on his teachers. When she was eventually persuaded to join in the home reading scheme it took only two weeks for his teachers to see changes in Terry. He became much more confident in his approach to his work and in his relationships with peers, and he more readily attempted the work given to him. After five weeks his mother commented to teachers on how much her relationship with Terry had improved. It took nearly six months for him to make any real strides with reading, but after a three-year period of standing still, this was great progress.

Another group of parents who worry teachers are those who continue to use 'wrong' methods, despite advice from the school. Such parents are rare when a school has sold its scheme well, but they do exist. Where teachers believe that this is happening, they need to liaise closely with the parents, trying to persuade them to change over a period of time. What must never be forgotten is that many parents already hear their children read;[6] by involving these parents directly with the school the worst that can happen is that there is no change in the methods they use, so schools have nothing to lose.

Children do have all kinds of pressures put on them by parents but in our experience, when the school and home work closely together, these pressures can be relieved. But the school must get its contribution across to parents clearly, and continue, often over a long period of time, to help those parents who particularly need its support.

Children whose parents aren't interested

Parents who genuinely aren't interested in their children's education must be quite hard to find; we haven't met any yet, though doubtless they must exist. Where the school takes the trouble to contact all its parents, the rate of take-up on the home reading schemes we have described is extremely high.

Even so, we must anticipate that there will always be a few who do not wish to co-operate with the school in this way, and all but the most determined teachers will probably feel that this is inevitable. The questions that remain to be answered are these:

How does a school ensure that the maximum number (if not all) of its parents are involved in the scheme?

What can be done about the children whose parents finally do *not* wish to be involved?

The first question is best answered by the concept of 'net spreading': if your first 'net' (the initial meeting) fails to 'catch' all the parents, there should be a series of others waiting to be employed. Further letters and a variety of follow-up meetings, contacting parents at the school gate, sending personal messages through the children, inviting parents to the school for individual talks with the class teacher or head, asking the school's education welfare officer to call on the parents for a chat about the school's new scheme – all these make for a progressively finer 'mesh'. Parents may be able to meet you only at unusual hours – one school suggests dropping in at 9.45 a.m. for a cup of coffee. The telephone should not be forgotten either, though this may be felt to be too invasive by some parents. Where parents cannot speak English, taking the trouble to find an interpreter can make all the difference.

Peer-group pressure from the children can also be used to encourage the apparently uninterested parent to join the scheme. One infant school set up a 'Book bug club', with all the children who were reading at home wearing special badges saying 'I'm a book bug'. In this particular school the idea worked very well, bringing in many parents whose children had nagged them into joining the scheme so they could have a badge like all the others! Once the school was satisfied, however, that the maximum possible number of parents was participating (having used all other possible ways to encourage them in), the teachers made sure that every child who wanted to join became a 'book bug'. Once the whole school was in the club, it had fulfilled its purpose. As the school recognized, this sort of idea has to be used with discretion, or schools themselves will fall into the same kind of 'pressurizing' as teachers may fear from some parents. But, carefully handled, peer-group pressures can promote a scheme very successfully.

So there is a great variety of ways to bring parents in. Yet another, not previously mentioned, is home visiting by teachers. We have left this for separate discussion, largely because home visiting is an area that may need sensitive handling. Clearly such visits can be valuable: when the CUES researchers[1] went into people's homes, they sometimes found reasons why parents could not visit schools, of which the schools themselves were unaware. Home visits are time-consuming, but usually productive in terms of new insights and improved relationships. Indeed, some schools find these visits so important that they incorporate at least one visit to each home during the school year, which means a big effort for the teachers. On the other hand, home visits can be intrusive and possibly unwelcome. It is not generally good practice to 'drop in' on parents on a casual basis, or for individual teachers to make visits without consultation within the school. This topic is worthy of full discussion in a staff meeting to decide whether and how it should be done, and who can do it most appropriately. Perhaps the most important point to remember about home visits is that a parent should always have the option of saying 'no' to a visit by a teacher.

It is more difficult to answer the question about how to look after the child whose parents really do not wish to participate. It is all very well for teachers to decide to relax the pressure and leave well alone; and, of course, one has no right to insist where an idea is unwelcome. But when most children are being heard reading at home, uninvolved children can feel left out. Sometimes this has been pointed out to us as though it were a serious reason for not implementing a PACT scheme at all, and although we find it impossible to agree with a point of view that suggests the majority should miss so much for the sake of a few, we agree that the matter should be taken very seriously. The answer is perhaps two-fold. First, the school must aim to show its enthusiasm for, and commitment to, home reading without suggesting undue pressure. This is a good deal easier said than done since, with the best intentions in the world, it is hard to prevent a child who feels left out *experiencing* pressure. Second, a determined effort must be made to find someone else for the child to read to, in circumstances as like home as possible. An older sibling, a family friend or neighbour, or an older pupil from the school might be asked to hear the child read, in the child's home or their own. Or another child's parents who are committed to home reading might invite the child to their home sometimes for a session.

Possibly a more common problem is the child who isn't interested. Here teachers – and parents – will be on familiar territory. In fact, though, where a school PACT scheme is working well, children tend to be swept along in the general enthusiasm, and the child who really does not want to read with his or her parents, at least occasionally, is a rarity. Where a child continues to be reluctant, the responses of parents and teachers will be dependent upon their knowledge of the individual child and the particular circumstances but this time at least they will have each other for support. Bear in mind also that there may be times (for instance, among top juniors) when it is quite appropriate to rebel against the idea of working closely with one's parents. Children who feel like this often find it acceptable, though, to have their parents read the same book separately and talk about it afterwards.

Children with special needs

Children with special needs, whether they are in a special school or an ordinary school, stand to benefit considerably from a PACT scheme, which at the very least promises them extra attention and care, and at best may be a real answer to certain of their needs. There is no reason why a special school should not run a PACT scheme. We know of some that do, and the only difficulty such a school is likely to experience is that of its wider catchment area, which may call for more home visiting. On the other hand, a special school usually has the advantage of much smaller numbers.

But the majority of children with special needs are in ordinary schools; and of these children by far the greater number are categorized as having learning or emotional difficulties, the latter often also associated with poor learning and under-achievement. In this context, Ted Glynn[14] in New Zealand and later in Birmingham, enabled the parents of a number of children who were very poor readers successfully to help their children, with results similar to that of the Haringey research. And it will be remembered that in the Haringey work, it seemed that children who were slow in learning to read gained especially from the help their parents gave them, to the extent that their parents seemed more useful than extra 'remedial' help in school.[2]

It is sometimes objected that the parents of children with emotional and learning difficulties are less likely to be able to help their children. The reason put forward is that this group might be expected to include a larger proportion of parents who could have a negative effect on their children's learning. Most teachers can point to children who they feel come into the 'special needs' category precisely because their needs are not being met adequately at home. The parents of these children, it is argued, may be especially prone to over-anxiety, denigration of a child's efforts, disorganization and so on. To this objection our reply can only be that in such cases any negative effects are presumably operating anyway, and perhaps only improvement can come from helping the parents to set up structured and enjoyable learning times, with steady support and advice from the child's teacher. Ted Glynn felt that much of the success of his work came from the fact that a simple, structured system was offered to the parents, laying particular stress on relaxation and enjoyment, and suggesting approximate rules of thumb, such as how long to wait before giving a child a word and when to point to a relevant cue. Parents responded extremely well to this: they lost much of their anxiety and many of them taught their children with considerable skill. It looks as though such collaboration may be an important way in to breaking the vicious circle so familiar to the 'remedial' teacher.

The 'under-fives' and the 'over-elevens'

No one questions the importance of a parent to a very young child's learning.[15,16] By the age of five, virtually all children have been taught a tremendous amount by their parents, including the important skill of language. Traditionally, professionals have tended to involve parents in many aspects of very young children's learning; but often they have shied from the prospect of involving them in the early stages of reading itself.

The Bullock Report unequivocally states that parents should be helped to prepare their child for learning to read (see chapter 2), and that schools have a responsibility to ensure that children and parents can see and select from a wide variety of books (7.1 and 7.5). The report gives examples of how parents can help their children to see reading as purposeful and enjoyable, without it becoming just an exercise in identifying shapes and sounds.

Parents do try to help their children with reading before they start school, and they can do much that would help their child to understand what reading is all about: which way up a book is read, where it starts and where it ends, that print goes from left to right and is made up of words and letters, and so on. But more than this, they can encourage their child to get a great deal of enjoyment from books.

Much of what has been said elsewhere in this book also applies to the under-fives. But there are differences, a crucial one being that much time is spent by parents reading to their children. Most parents will have experienced their child's enjoyment and their own frustration at reading *Goldilocks and the Three Bears* for the sixteenth time in succession, and it is not always easy for parents to appreciate how much children will gain from this. Nor do they necessarily recognize that learning to read is not just about decoding symbols on a page. Nursery classes, playgroups and toddler groups are ideal forums for discussing the elements of good practice with parents, and we have included an example in chapter 7 of a nursery class operating a PACT scheme. This particular scheme has led to a considerable increase in the number of parents reading to their children and in the total amount of time they spend reading to them.

It is at secondary age that the biggest split between parents and teachers usually exists. Cynics point out that liaison between teacher and teacher is quite difficult enough in a large comprehensive school, without adding to that liaison between teacher and parent. The cynics are quite wrong. We have been able to refer to a number of successful PACT secondary schemes in this book, and a detailed account of one scheme will be found in chapter 7, page 88. The use of 'paired reading' with children of secondary age who have reading difficulties is becoming extensive (see chapter 9), and many English and special needs departments have set up formal PACT reading schemes catering for children of all abilities.

Undoubtedly, the size and structure of secondary schools create difficulties not faced by primary schools, but the success of those schemes already operating demonstrates parental willingness to continue to be involved when their children reach secondary age. One major obstacle for parents is the subject-based curriculum, with its concomitant department boundaries, which makes liaison between teachers and parents at best cumbersome. We should like to see teachers from all areas of the curriculum involved and not just those from the English and special needs departments working with a few interested others. Schools can do much by the judicious use of letters home, by having open evenings on particular subject areas, and by holding discussion groups on topics that interest parents. But if parents are to help older children educationally on a day-to-day basis, schools and parents will need to find common ground that is capable of bridging departmental boundaries (see chapter 10).

The 'under-fives' and the 'over-elevens' have as much to gain as any other children from PACT schemes. Liaison with the parents of both these groups may be more difficult – the former because not all of them attend a nursery school, the latter because of the inevitably complex organization of a secondary school – and it may be impossible for teachers to work with every parent. Nevertheless, the examples of successful practice we do have should encourage schools to overcome the difficulties and to try to work with the great majority of parents.

6

Questions parents ask

It is as well to be prepared for the kinds of questions you may be asked at open meetings, or indeed at any time. The questions in this chapter have emerged frequently, and usually early on, in parent-teacher dialogue. Often they have been asked at the first meeting. We have included the sorts of replies that might be suitable at a public forum, but all the questions deserve to be talked through more fully and personally with the parents whose concern they are. The suggestions we give are not intended to be exhaustive, but to highlight points we think it important not to overlook.

But my child can read already – so how does this affect me?

This question calls for quite a full answer. There are sure to be other parents listening who are in the same position, and it is essential to let them know that the school does not see help with reading as applying only to the early stages, but that you are concerned with the child's development as a fluent reader, able to learn from his or her own reading and to discuss it critically. So this can be an opportunity to talk about all the different activities that are part of good reading practice.

You could suggest a wider range of materials than the child may be used to – newspapers and magazines, reference books and encyclopedias, paperback versions of TV serials, poetry and plays, instruction manuals and recipes. Relate this breadth of reading material to the idea of reading for different purposes – for pleasure, for information, to follow instructions, to understand new ideas. Parents can help a child to a deeper understanding of what he or she is reading, through discussion and questions (properly timed, of course, and not used intrusively to ruin a good story). Point out that however simple the level of a story, talking about it can lead the child toward critical thinking and deeper understanding, from the simplest factual questions: 'What happened when Red Riding Hood got to the cottage?' to 'I wonder what would have happened if the woodcutter hadn't come . . .' and 'I think if I were Red Riding Hood I'd have . . . what would you have felt/done/said?' Parents can help children to skim and scan, rather than always plodding through a book reading every word; to reflect on a text, and to predict; to decide whether the writer has told the story well, or described a process clearly. Parents may find the terms 'study skills' or 'learning skills' helpful, suggesting as they do much wider horizons than simple reading.

A good concrete suggestion that embodies all the above is for parent and child to find a topic both are interested in, choose reading material on the subject and find ways of understanding it better: through using the library, going on visits, watching relevant television programmes – and eventually progressing to more difficult texts. Encourage the use of a good dictionary, perhaps one that gives derivations if this would be helpful, or fun. Can the child use contents pages, indexes, diagrams? Can he or she make full use of the public library, via the subject/ author index, the use of classification numbers – and through the confidence to ask for the librarian's help when it is needed?

One important thing parents can sometimes forget is that a child who can read well is still a child; the fact that some children are good readers doesn't mean that adults should stop reading to them. And a child who reads well may need to read an easy book sometimes, for the enjoyment and emotional security that it can provide – even highly educated adults like to regress with a silly novel occasionally.

Above all, stress the importance of a good working alliance and the way sharing interests through reading broadens children's understanding. If parents find reading enjoyable, then the most important thing they can do is to pass this experience on to their children.

My child is behind with his reading – if the teachers find it difficult to help him, how can I?

This question turns up regularly – sometimes phrased less politely! One answer (see chapter 2, page 11) is that parents may actually be more likely than teachers to find they can help a child who has difficulty with reading. Talk about the importance of the close emotional relationship between parent and child, and how this can speed the learning process; and point out, via some quick arithmetic, just how little time a teacher can give to each child, compared with a parent's ten or fifteen minutes a day.

In the way of practical help, suggest games that could be played at home (e.g. word bingo or a cloze game where children fill in missing words or phrases), explaining the particular value of games to a child with reading problems – namely that they're fun and so don't seem too much like hard work, and also that they have a useful repetitive, reinforcing function. When you recommend a game, try to explain just how it is designed to help. There are booklets and pamphlets available, which give ideas for games that can easily be made and played at home (e.g. *Hip Pocket Spelling Games* series, New York, Harcourt Brace Jovanovich, 1983).

Remind parents that we no longer insist on precise accuracy when it comes to understanding what the book is saying, so that if a child makes a good guess, he or she should be praised for trying to get at the writer's meaning. This should take some of the anxiety out of listening to a child's inaccuracies and give more opportunities for parents to make children feel pleased with their own efforts, so that both have a sense of achievement rather than failure.

If reading difficulties persist, the school may be prepared to support the parent through the 'paired reading' technique (see chapter 9) but remember that this means giving up extra time on your part, because it needs close monitoring.

And finally, don't be afraid to stress again the importance of parents and children just talking and listening to each other. Quote Lawrence (see chapter 8), who achieved improved reading results using nothing else.

The fact is, I can't read very well myself – so how can I help?

You may find this confession made more frequently than you might expect (though perhaps not in the open meeting itself), because parents can see a real point in admitting to being unable to read when it looks as if that could put their own children at a disadvantage.

You can legitimately reassure any parent, however poor his or her reading ability may be, that being unable to read need not prevent anyone from helping a child to read. Reading is about understanding and enjoyment, and the job of the adult is to promote these, through listening. It isn't necessary to be able to read well yourself to be able to say 'Hold on – that doesn't make sense – try that again' or 'I liked that bit, didn't you?' We always find, too, that non-reading parents are cheered when they are told about Lawrence's work! (see chapter 8).

Parents who want to help their children are often motivated

to improve their own reading. Point out that there is a good chance of this happening if they hear their children read regularly, especially when they have young children with easy books to read. You could add that the experience of having their parents trying to learn at the same time can be a helpful one for children too. It is very useful, in case you are asked, to be ready with accurate information about local provisions for adult literacy (who to ring, what evening, time, etc.). Vague recommendations, as we all know from experience, rarely get followed up.

We speak Punjabi at home – I can speak English but not read it

While this may be a real difficulty for parents, the possession of a second language can be an advantage for children, and parents should be encouraged to see their mother tongue in this light. We know that what matters most in learning to read is what the child brings to reading: that is, language skills (and implicit in this, conceptual structures) sufficiently developed for the child's understanding to match the writer's intention. This development can take place through the medium of any language, so use of the mother tongue can be encouraged, since it is via this language that parents will be more fluent and can convey more complex meaning to their children. When you explain this to parents, ask them to talk, tell stories and use books in the mother tongue at home. They could also use the simple reading books that are now available in various languages, sometimes with English translations (e.g. *The Snowy Day*, published by Bodley Head). An alternative is to use books which contain space for texts in other languages, such as *The Terraced House Books*, published by Methuen.

Point out the advantage to the parents of helping their children with reading, and so themselves gaining more knowledge of written English. Have details ready of local classes in English as a second language; and it may be useful to be informed about local clubs and associations for different ethnic groups. From this point on, most of what has been said to non-reading parents is also relevant.

I've got five children . . . !

This is typical of the many practical difficulties some families face. You cannot, of course, explore the family circumstances in detail in an open meeting, but you do need to suggest ways in which the problem can begin to be tackled. A few well-placed questions should enable you to put forward some useful strategies. It may be impossible to hear children read as often as a smaller family could manage, but other members of the family might be recruited to help – big brother or sister, grandparents, even a neighbour. In one large family, a reading 'chain' was set up, with each child reading to the one above in age. Careful thought must be given to organization: can the twins be fitted in on Mondays and Thursdays, after cartoon time but before supper? Do they get on well enough to read together, sitting on either side of the adult and taking turns? And don't forget the evening Dad gets in early, and the weekends.

It's sums my child needs help with more than reading. Should I try to help with that?

Yes, there are many possibilities, especially those that arise in everyday experiences like shopping and sorting, matching and counting. Help your child to check the change, to guess whether the cupboard will fit into the space and then check it, to match articles correctly as in laying the table, to make a graph of the football results. Avoid any anxiety or pressure, of course. Try to bring in maths where the child wants to know the answer for his or her own purposes, so that getting the right answer is genuinely rewarding.

Guessing intelligently is almost as important in maths as in reading. Encourage children to estimate things before they make a calculation, so that they don't come up with impossible answers because they don't see a connection between the sum and the reality.

And 'sums' nowadays are very much about understanding mathematical concepts, for which language and reading are centrally important. Have you *talked* about some of the problems in the maths books and made sure your child reads them fluently and understands them?

I'm a house-parent at a children's home – aren't you forgetting about the children in care?

Not at all – everything that applies to parents, and especially to those with large families, applies to careworkers. One school had five or six children in care in a local children's home, which was very enthusiastic about the link between the home and the school provided by the PACT scheme. It was felt that the evening reading times were particularly valuable to children and careworkers alike, providing an atmosphere much like that of an ordinary home, and giving an opportunity for workers to show the children they cared about them, through an activity that went beyond the usual evening pursuits. Staff comments showed how pleased they were with the role the scheme afforded them, and how they felt it gave them new and close contact with the children. The school was asked to make a point of monitoring the children's reading ages, and indeed these all showed improvement.

I thought *school* was the place where children were supposed to be educated?

Here is just the chance you have been waiting for to advertise this book!

7

Examples of current practice

In this chapter four teachers working in different educational settings write about their own work with parents. Any example demonstrating PACT in practice necessarily reflects the school's and its teachers' individuality, and those we have chosen certainly do this. They display, too, the richness and the broadening effects of parental involvement extending beyond the boundaries of reading. This broadening is inevitable when people are actually working together, and we believe it is the mark of good parent-teacher collaboration. Indeed, in our second example the PACT reading scheme forms only a minor part of the co-operative effort between teachers and the local community.

All our contributors work in inner-city schools in which they have had to meet and overcome a wide range of problems, including many that we have already touched on. They work with different age-groups, and each had different reasons for starting a PACT scheme.

Elizabeth Doak is a primary school headteacher. She and her staff were the pioneers of the first PACT scheme in the large junior school of which she was then the headteacher.

Iris Walkinshaw, headteacher of a large infant school, shows how PACT has become part of her school's way of life, as she and her staff endeavour to make the school an integral part of the surrounding community.

Angela Jefferis, a nursery class teacher, piloted a PACT scheme in which parents read to their children, and this is now part of her weekly routine.

Phil Gryce helped a comprehensive school to develop a PACT scheme for first-year children while working as a special needs support teacher.

I   PRACTICE IN A JUNIOR SCHOOL: A PARTNERSHIP WITH PARENTS

Elizabeth Doak

Looking back, several separate strands of development in our home reading scheme seem very clear. It is easy to use hindsight to improve on reality but I will try to avoid it by reminding myself at the outset what exceedingly hard work the scheme was for everyone involved. It was not just in the planning and preparation stages, not solely in the frantic exercise of the launch – a period of about three weeks – but in the continuous daily practice of monitoring, talking, recording, meeting, supporting and yet more planning. Maintenance and revitalization were crucial factors from the first week of the scheme's operation. A few preliminary factors, I believe, are of overriding importance in the success of the first eighteen months.

A staff that had become accustomed to, successful at and found rewarding the practice of continuous, positive discussion of its work is the first factor. People in our staffroom were used to listening to colleagues and finding their opinions interesting and informative. Discussion of one's strategies, regard for others' views, a lack of any expectation of adverse criticism in relating one's current concerns, failures and successes – all this had become part of our daily staffroom talk. A very determined ethos had grown, and was firmly sustained, which held all children in regard, felt deep concern about their problems in learning and behaviour and took pains to find better strategies to help them. This was our overriding direction. It sounds, perhaps, earnest, studied, commonplace, obvious, as I write it but it was in fact supportive, lively and friendly. The habit, then, of positive discussion on real issues to do with school policy, curriculum and children's needs was well established before the home reading project began. People were used to taking joint decisions and implementing them rigorously.

Development of children's language had been the predominant goal of the school and over several years much discussion and policy-making had centred on this. With an energetic and knowledgeable postholder responsible for language development, eager to make policy with teachers and capable of implementing it firmly, a good deal of progress had been made. Some of it showed in a lessened need for remedial reading programmes and, with the support of the Pitfield Project, we were withdrawing fewer children from classes. Alongside this, there had been the careful, systematic purchase and organization of resources over several years to suit the needs of the children currently being taught in the school. However obvious this may sound, it is not something that happens without strenuous efforts on somebody's part, and not in the short term either. We had evolved two good, well-arranged and attractive school libraries (our school having four floors in use) with a central catalogue for book and non-book resources designed for children to use unaided, after some instruction and practice. A lively library corner was provided in every classroom. A bookshop and a large bookstore where sets, series and supplementaries were colour-coded for readability on a junior-adjusted Cliff Moon-style system[13] completed a complex but accessible supply of good, up-to-date reading material.

The school's recognition of the importance of parents' interest and concern for their children had produced, if a little patchily, a certain openness and relaxation in the school. Talking to parents and, more importantly, listening to them, was a daily practice. Certain routines made this possible. If they wished, parents could wait for or with their children in the playground and then come directly into school to speak to the head or a teacher about a small or large issue without an appointment or any need to break through difficult procedures. Teachers collected children from the playground to begin each session and saw them out at the session's end, so that frequent exchanges of small talk and minor but necessary information flowed freely for those parents who collected and delivered their children. The point was firmly pressed home, through letters and at meetings, that we would prefer to hear of and sort out together small problems as soon as they arose, rather than wait until they had become serious and worrying issues.

Frequent relaxed open days and evenings had evolved where children showed visitors their school and their own work within it. With no necessity to have a formal meeting with the head or a teacher, more parents came more frequently, and sometimes family groups with gran or an older brother and sister would take the place of a parent who could not fit in with our arrangements. Cups of tea and a place to sit, a chance to see the bookshop, look at school journey slides or watch a rounders match were part of the usual year's planning. Frequently parents helped with particular school curriculum events, sports, plays, outings and school journeys. School fairs and jumble sales depended almost entirely on their help and general organization.

So a certain area of satisfactory and useful relationships existed which supported and enriched the life of the school and the children's experiences. Parents came for help with increasing frequency, often initiating discussion of children's problems. In earlier years we had had to 'send' for them, wasting a good deal of time and energy in getting to know each other's views and opinions before a shared understanding of the child's problem and a joint decision on the next steps to take could be reached. Suggestions for interviews with the educational psychologist, an appointment at a child guidance clinic, a placement in the 'nurture group', came from parents to us, since they had become aware through talking with other parents, staff and neighbours that these were positive and frequently successful ways of gaining help with problems that were concerning them. This was a development that we had noted with pleasure and enthusiasm.

To start with, then, we had the skills, attitudes, people and materials all in good shape. What made us begin? I think a process of natural development stirred by one or two catalysts. When the Haringey[6] and CUES research[1] was presented at our weekend staff conference it spoke to the nagging concern we had experienced for several years when reviewing the area of parental communication and involvement. Writing a pilot annual review that year had brought this feeling to a head. We connected with some parents well; with most intermittently; but with a fair proportion never. We realized that we were not responding sufficiently to the real, if usually unexpressed, concern of all the parents: the desire to continue to be effective in their children's intellectual development and daily learning. All the work at fairs and jumble sales did not advance this need one iota and we had seemed, traditionally, content to leave it so.

We began nine weeks of planning and preparation in which staff took part, shared in decision-making and moved on to the detailed, almost pernickety, development of strategies, materials and organization. And this painstaking approach was a most influential factor in the success of our scheme. Every imagined pitfall was sought out in advance, responses to probable questions and problems were prepared. Our preparations laid down the first basic outlines of our intentions – to deal with all children and parents in the school, to involve all staff, to lay down broad areas of agreement over how the scheme would function, to decide on jobs to be done and split into small groups, twos or threes, to carry out the work. We decided quickly on one large initial meeting to launch the scheme, to be followed by one or two meetings each term to maintain the reality of parents' involvement with us in the school and provide a platform for continuing discussion and development. We distinguished all information sent from school to parents by using one colour, and heading it distinctively with a simple slogan 'Reading – help us to help your child'. The main outlines of guidance for parents were agreed, stressing enjoyment and relaxation, and making sure that short, shared reading times did not interfere with the needs of parents and children to choose other activities, favourite TV programmes, playing with friends, or having a cup of tea after a hard day's work. By insisting on a flexible approach we aimed to avoid pressure, anxiety and the relegating of the reading process to the status of another chore.

We took great pains over what appeared to be small and simple tasks. The initial letter to parents inviting them to the meeting was planned and written by several members of staff, who had pointed out that my letters home (that I thought were very friendly, clear and informative) often turned out to be lengthy, confused, directive and patronizing – ah well, it was a learning time for us all! The final letter was a model of clear, uncluttered information in the form of an invitation and I still refer to it occasionally when I find a letter to parents is running into more than three paragraphs!

The staff preparing the booklet did an excellent job, packing a mass of information into a few paragraphs, using pictures to convey attitudes and atmosphere and, most importantly, avoiding patronizing phraseology and jargon.

I had asked that we give parents the right (generally neglected) and the machinery to report to us on their child's progress. We wanted the parents to see themselves as teachers and also to be aware that we saw them clearly in this role and would value their comments on the work they did at home. Again, the teachers who undertook this area of work produced something that proved remarkably effective. The report card became the significant thread that bound the scheme together – it had the effect of providing the child with the main responsibility for maintaining a conversation between his parents and his teacher, on a roughly three-times-a-week basis. The growing awareness of children of the reality of their mother or father exchanging messages with their teacher about them and their work was noticeable.

As the weeks went by the gradual lessening of tension in home-school relationships was easily felt about the school. The awful nerve-wracking ordeal, particularly for a young, inexperienced and often very tired teacher, of the first open evening of the year, meeting thirty, maybe forty or fifty parents – mostly for the first time – and trying to guess at and satisfy all their anxieties and often unknown attitudes about the teacher's work with their child, all in the space of two or three hours after a long day's work, has always seemed to me some sort of refined masochism. Yet we go on doing it. But there is less need to feel anxious about meeting a mother who jotted down a cheery 'Thanks for all your help' on a reading card the previous week; or a dad who, on hearing his son read for what one can only suppose was the very first time, simply wrote 'STREWTH!' across the card and became noticeably more appreciative of the work of teachers from that date. It's good to see the faces of the people you've been exchanging wry jokes with on their child's determination to finish every Viking saga ever published; to exchange mutual admiration for a victory jointly won to turn a reluctant reader into an avid bookworm. So parents and teachers were more often meeting on a basis of shared knowledge and information about one of the most potentially worrying areas of primary children's learning, and more often with a predisposition to work together in a mutually supportive way towards the child's progress.

The card also acted as a great source of information between all of us in school. Parents' comments on the content, or quality, of the book sent home were taken seriously: in all but the smallest school we cannot hope to know every book, particularly if we are fortunate enough to be able to pride ourselves on the quantity, variety and breadth of provision we can make! So it is to be expected that occasionally we retain or acquire a book of unsuitable, offensive or simply out-of-date views or information. Equally valuable information flowed in about books that were simply boring and, even more usefully, those that appealed to child and adult, for us to remember, re-order and use in the classroom. Teachers temporarily attached to a class or group, or seeing children just once or twice a week, had a ready insight into the child's ability and stage of development in reading as well as in their range of reading.

And there was the inestimable value, quite unplanned, but rapidly and naturally capitalized on by parents and teachers, of an ease of communication that had not existed before. As I reviewed a class's cards I was amazed at the range of messages that flowed about. It is true that this was much more a feature of some classes than others: so the teacher's attitude was clearly the crucial factor. Lost plimsolls were pursued relentlessly with cryptic phrases cropping up day after day – 'I've even looked behind the big cupboard'. 'Never mind he'll just have to hop.' 'Eureka! You'll never guess where!' – left me agog for the answer. Some long conversations developed – *Watership Down* was being read, with interest, persistence and some tremendous parental support. 'We're going to see the film in the holiday.' 'You'll love it, I've been.' 'I like the record too.' 'So do we. Perhaps we'll get it this weekend.' Some forceful views were expressed: 'It seems to me that this book bears very little resemblance to life in Hackney. If Mummy could get away from servicing the family wouldn't life be more interesting.' *Teacher*: 'I couldn't agree with you more. I've sent Ian back to choose "something else" (anything else).' *Parent*: 'A much nicer book, but more difficult.' To the same parent later: 'Quite difficult but Ian would like to read it.' *Parent*: 'Ian and I read this book together. An interesting story.' News of dentist appointments, special occasions, apologies for lateness, plans to visit school, attend meetings, help with cooking or a play flowed back and forth. Hints were dropped: 'Sorry I didn't see you at the meeting last night', greetings exchanged, and mutual congratulations offered on efforts being made and sustained.

For me, to spend a day going through each class's cards was an occasion to discover more about the children's lives, the teachers' work, the parents' care and concerns than I might otherwise learn in a whole term.

Did we achieve any particular goals? Oh yes. We grew in knowledge and awareness of parents, and gained a much higher regard for them both as parents and as effective teachers. There was the mutual satisfaction of a job done well in which everyone played a continuing and vital role. We learned more about children's books in two or three terms than we might have done in our whole teaching career so far. And, of course, there was the sheer gratification of improved literacy levels in the school, enhancing everyone's ability to work well.

For me, several things were of overall importance in the long term. There was the deep professional satisfaction of seeing large numbers of good children's books which had been bought, often years earlier, in the hope rather than the certainty that older juniors would read and enjoy them, disappearing from class and library shelves and seeing their titles down on individual children's cards with little messages: 'She enjoyed this'; 'We'd like another by this author please if you've got any'. There was the equally deep satisfaction of not needing to re-order the large quantities of pre-reader and emergent reader material that had been the daily bread of most of the first and second years. It is warming to work closely with enthusiastic, caring and hardworking colleagues to develop something that works in the children's interest and will enhance their opportunities for learning in the long term, and to recognize that now we have the vital, effective and willing help of so many new colleagues previously shamefully disregarded – the great army of parents, brothers, sisters, grans and neighbours who, with a little help and a lot of encouragement, are such effective teachers. Reading levels in the school rose considerably over all age-ranges and abilities. Books at a higher level were needed in greater quantities.

The most difficult area of all to measure and assess, the overall quality of written work in the school, seemed to me to have improved noticeably over a period of four terms. Children wrote with a more fluent and surer grasp of the rhythms of written English, with a sounder approach to sentence construction and using wider and more precise vocabulary, relying less on stereotypes of phrasing than previously. Parents felt we had made an effort to answer their needs; they felt closer to the school, its teachers and aims, and took the trouble to express it, both in attitudes and in words. We answered their request to move on to other aspects of children's learning outside the classroom, through mathematics, and were rewarded again; and again we were reminded of the parent's understanding and knowledge of our work, when our fears that there could be vociferous demands for a formal maths homework scheme proved entirely unfounded, and our advice and information about games and other activities to reinforce mathematical concepts were accepted, with no one demanding that we 'teach them to say their tables and then they'll get on all right'.

II PRACTICE IN AN INFANT SCHOOL: THE HUMAN FACE OF PACT

Iris Walkinshaw

In our school PACT means more than getting parents to help children at home with reading. It means involving ourselves with parents as a way of getting *them* involved with the school and their children's total education. We realized that making the school somewhere where everyone in the family had a say and a place would forge closer lasting links, and would offer natural opportunities for contact, consultation and co-operation. We decided on certain strategies; others developed as offshoots, as you will see as you read on.

Access to building – keeping open house

I was brought up on a tiny West Indian island. I started my teaching career there and because I knew all of the parents as neighbours and friends I did not find it difficult here to think of parents as individual personalities with whom to deal. It was because of this that the whole policy developed of allowing parents and friends free access to the school at any time. There is absolutely no inconvenient time to arrive. Whatever is going on at the moment, all visitors are asked to take part or join in. The staff and I may not have time to talk with them at length, but they are encouraged to wander around the building and to observe and absorb the atmosphere of the school.

Access to staff

No appointments are needed to see me, especially if parents are worried. Parents of five to seven-year-olds want immediate answers, comfort, sympathy and reassurance. If I am out, the school is organized to provide cover so that my deputy or the class teacher can be available. Appointments are only made if a lengthy discussion is anticipated. This is to prevent 'double booking' and disappointment. As the head I aim to be available at the most crucial parts of the school day – when the children come to school and at home time.

In the mornings I am on hand to greet (informally) parents and children from the time I enter the playground until a good fifteen minutes or so after the bell, when I 'tut-tut' at latecomers – who still get a smile, a little gossip and of course a scold if they're habitual offenders, or commiserations if a domestic hiccup caused the unpunctuality. It is during this time that I get filled in on domestic matters, news of illness, clinic appointments, broken nights with ailing babies and the like. Children tell me who has read with them, show off new clothes. Parents tell me informally of any apprehension about or dissatisfaction with children's progress. Briefer versions are aired in the classrooms, of course, but with twenty-five or so children waiting even the most self-centred parent soon realizes a teacher's limitations as a listener under these circumstances. This is also the time when I start dropping hints of proposed changes, plans, events, meetings; when I in turn listen to suggestions, answer questions, seek and give advice (not only on school matters but on any other subject which the parents and I deem necessary or relevant).

At home time I aim to be in the hall or playground to chat about the day, say goodnight, talk about circular letters and coming events – in fact this session is like the morning's, but now I tend to concentrate attention on the parents I did not see at the beginning of the day.

The school as a place for the entire family

The staff and I are committed to the idea that the school belongs to the family. Anything that goes on is seen as a starting-point and a focus for work within the framework of the school curriculum. This is why we actively encourage and use the involvement of the entire family.

Parents and toddlers are welcome at all times. Having a baby to look after does not exclude the mother or dad from helping. We ask for babies to be brought in so our children can observe them at play, and play with them or watch them being given a bath or feed. During a project to highlight equal opportunities for girls and boys a dad changed his month-old baby's nappy. Even pets play their part. They too are brought in to show off teeth, behaviour (good or disruptive!), paws, coats and the like. Relatives – aunts, uncles, cousins, grandparents – and child-minders and family friends are highly valued as part of the school. We see them as important, especially in reinforcing the positive attitude to school which it is so necessary for a child to develop and maintain. The more adults involved, the greater 'status' and security the child seems to acquire. This is invariably reflected in the child's behaviour and work.

Parents as partners

Our parents have organized a Parents, Teachers and Friends Group. They felt that, to be more effective, a formal group should exist, with a committee. Thus the PTFG was formed and is now fully active, involving itself with the running of the school, organizing meetings, crèches, arranging fêtes and other fund-raising events. Even as individuals, parents have now learnt that they can make suggestions or question any practice or decision made by the staff. They are actively encouraged to do this, and are sure of a chance for discussion or a listening ear. We work on the premise that parents have a vested interest in the school and without them there would be no school! At the same time we emphasize that whatever we do must be for the benefit of every child's education and that all children have a right to equal opportunities within the framework of the school.

Parents' obligations

When I admit a child to the school there are certain things I emphasize. I like to think that, even with parents I am seeing for the first time, a relationship is being formed which will be strengthened as the child goes through the school.

1 I tell parents that they are expected to share fully with us the responsibility of continuing the education of their child. I draw attention to the child's present achievements and remind them that these were learnt at home. I then finalize the argument by asking them to continue this valuable work to the benefit of the child, themselves and the staff.

2 The best way, I urge, is to get to know us and what goes on in school. This can only happen by visiting as frequently as possible. I challenge parents to come as often as they can. Some go away quite startled after I declare bluntly that if they do not visit me, then I will assume that they want me to visit them, so if I am not welcome they'd better be seen around. I do carry out my threat (or promise) and fortunately I have not yet been assaulted!

3 I also remind them that we have regular parents' meetings, at which many issues are raised and discussed – proposals for changes in policy, areas of the curriculum, the school building, organization, etc. That they are required to attend as

many as possible is made quite clear. In letters sent home there is a tear-off slip which states:

I/We can come to the meeting.
Sorry I/We cannot come to the meeting because . . .

Besides putting them on the spot and making them think again about their reason for not attending, it helps us to plan another meeting when these reasons are analysed. The children are also encouraged to join with the staff and me in harassing their parents, with a verbal bombardment of the issues outlined in the circular, up to the last minute before the commencement of any meeting.

4   I also put before parents the powerful argument that they have a wealth of talent which could be invaluable to the school. No one, I remind them, is without something to offer. Parents who may only be able to listen are of use to children to whom no one ever listens.

5   One of our parents found his strength lay in reclaiming our school garden from the wilderness, and keeping it well stocked with flowers and vegetables in season! Parents whose talents lie in other directions have taken over various functions in the school, for example:

Running the school lending library – three parents currently organize and look after this. They now have a 'budget' and, in consultation with children, parents and staff, order books to supplement and replace stock.

Mother-tongue work – the bilingual parents have organized themselves to come in to read, tell stories and talk to and listen to children who speak their language.

Helping in the classroom – many parents come on a regular basis to hear children read or to read to them. Others supervise small groups in activities directed by the teacher or suggested by themselves. Still others take small groups for cooking. This is invaluable as parents tend to find some food typical of their culture which fits in with class topics. What with johnny cakes, curried vegetables, jam tarts, tomato sandwiches, stewed chicken, wholemeal bread, egg custard, scrambled eggs on toast, chappati and curry, biriani rice, pop corn, boiled green banana, sweet potato, yams, dasheen, not to mention coconuts (milk and meat) and sugarcane, we are hard put to retain our figures!

Accompanying us on visits is another way in which parents help. Many also come back to help with follow-up work based on the visit.

Beautification of the school! – parents are deeply interested in the surroundings in which their children have to work and learn. They help to mend toys, to rearrange furniture, to see that the playground is free from litter – but their *pièce de résistance* is the splendid playground mural opened by the mayor of our borough. The idea was conceived by a small group in the PTFG who, after discussion with the staff and committee, set the ball rolling and enlisted the aid of folk and organizations in the community, together with our own children, parents and staff – and produced a new, colourful, bright environment for us where before everything was dull and grey.

As mentioned above, one parent keeps the school garden in tip-top condition. Others have obtained tubs and filled them with seasonal plants to beautify the playground.

Extending the school's function for the entire family and community

We felt we needed involvement to extend even beyond the children on our roll and the parents who bring them. These are the tactics we employed:

1   We made provisions for toddlers and escorts, i.e. mums, dads, grandparents, other relatives and child-minders, on one afternoon a week. Toddlers play with toys under the supervision of escorts. Some of the older children join them and spend part of the session with them. At 3.00 p.m. some go with siblings to classrooms for a story.

2   We circulate child-minders, traders and prospective parents when special events are taking place, and about functions and events in the school as well as ordinary news.

3   Toddlers are invited to parties, shows and special assemblies. At the Christmas party, they have their own visit from Father Christmas.

4   We have affiliations with a local playgroup who send a group one morning a week to work and play with the under-fives class. In addition, when parents come to collect older children at the end of the day, they freely choose books from the shelves to read with the toddlers in the hall. It is not unusual to see parents at the cupboard with older children choosing books to take home, some quietly reading with toddlers, with yet others having a quiet gossip or reading the notices on the parent's noticeboard, tidying a display where busy fingers have been, or even breastfeeding.

5   Old age pensioners are the guests of honour at our harvest festival. Those who can attend are made welcome and, after the special assembly, are regaled with refreshments including their beloved cups of tea. Some linger on for the entire day, having school dinner and enjoying the company of our delightful pupils. The gifts the children bring are distributed to the various grandparents or elderly neighbours whose names are sent in to be recipients of the food donated by parents. We also tell them of jumble sales, where good bargains can be picked up.

6   We are fortunate in having a street market nearby which provides a ready-made source for enriching and enlivening our school life. Many traders allow visits and take time for discussion and to answer questions. Some come in to give talks about their stock. They are also very ready to give whenever we have sales and fêtes, and we are often offered goods at competitive prices!

Providing useful services for our parents

1   We found that one of the most useful services we could provide was keeping a register of child-minders, and also one

of escorts to and from school. On admission, I have my book ready, to the relief of many hard-pressed parents to whom 9.15 and 3.30 are impossible times when their working day begins at 8.30 a.m. and ends at 5.00 p.m.

2   If a prospective parent comes seeking an early placement, the school provides information about local nursery schools, classes and playgroups. In many cases, to save harassed mums with small children a long walk, I telephone other schools on the spot to get current information about vacancies. This is often a great relief to them. I also tell them of our school's mums and toddlers group, and invite them to attend with babies and all.

3   We are fortunate enough to have a nurture unit. Parents are invited to breakfast or tea. Many birthdays are celebrated with parties at school. This all started when a family had to be given emergency shelter in a hotel and the child's birthday fell during this period. What could we do but let him have his celebrations at school? Now party food is prepared in cooking lessons – practical, educational and social, not to mention convenient for parents.

4   One distinct advantage some of the staff have is that we live locally and therefore have greater chances of meeting parents in an environment other than the school. If a child has been hurt at school I can easily visit in the evening when parents are calmer and more relaxed. Invariably these visits are really appreciated and parents often confess to feeling cared for, and say they feel their children are important to us as individuals. If (as there will be in the best-run school) there is any disagreement between school and parent, or parent and parent, I often try to visit at home. This tends to take the heat out of many situations which could flare up and mar the relationships in our school.

5   The staff are all geared up to take some of the burden off the shoulders of the already overloaded education welfare officer. We try to find out why children are absent, and give advice about domestic problems involving children and their welfare. We organize the collection of welfare clothing parcels

if mums have several small children and find it difficult to travel. When one mum was in the last weeks of pregnancy we organized an escort for her child to be taken for speech therapy at the local clinic. We also did this for a parent who would have lost her job if she had had to take time off to attend these sessions.

When I admit children I tell every parent of the provisions made by the education authority in case of need. Many are ignorant of these, others think they amount to charity, others again feel that to take advantage of them is scrounging and so is a cause for embarrassment. I have managed in all but a few cases to talk them out of this attitude, and to make them feel pride in a system which is there to provide the means to a full and trouble-free education for their children.

Parents and reading

We find that our practice of caring and sharing keeps up the momentum of PACT. More specifically, there are several things we do that are directly concerned with fostering reading.

1   We read to the children a great deal so that they become very familiar with books and so try to re-read them to themselves. We believe that this is one of the chief ways that children learn to read. We are careful in our selection of books, so that they appeal to all the children. As time in schools is at a premium our programme is immensely enhanced by the help given at home by the whole family.

2   Parents are often invited to share in topic work. I can call to mind the mums in one class who had to make a list of things they would have taken on the ark if they were Mrs Noah. On another occasion they had to compile a list of dishes they made with flour, and cook one of them for the school. Many said how much they enjoyed being part of what was going on. Yet others were asked to allow groups to visit their homes to help in a 'Homes' topic. They not only welcomed the groups but also laid on refreshments for the children. It is difficult to know whether the children's enthusiasm was chiefly for what they

learned about 'open fires' and how water gets in and out of a house, or for the splendid feasts provided!

3   At Christmas the children were given bags, in which they could carry books to and from home, inscribed with their names and the school reading logo. They are very proud of these. Parents think they are a marvellous idea. We do too!

They also have record cards which parents can choose to complete. Some parents and teachers find these unnecessary as they meet so often. In fact, one teacher said she felt really set up for the day by speaking with parents about the progress of 'homework' rather than by using these cards. Fair enough!

4   We insist that every child should be a member of the local library. I keep a supply of application cards for new admissions and also for siblings. For parents who say that the under-fives are too young to join the library, I gasp in horror, and talk dramatically about the wonderful books that are there for children of that age. This provokes discussion and most parents leave with a card, promising to visit the library as soon as possible.

5   Whenever I meet any child after school, part of our greeting is a talk about who will be reading with them that evening. The teachers do this in class as well – wall charts are made: 'People who read with me', and used in maths and language work. Reading with children at home has become a part of school lore and of home routine for almost all our families.

6   We have invested money in providing a good supply of new and relevant books for our children. They have a wide choice and really take pleasure in choosing their daily selection for home reading.

7   We also run a school lending library where they can obtain two books at whatever level they desire. These are changed on a weekly basis.

The entire school is organized to give parents a full share in planning and participating in their children's education. Literacy is the key to almost every subject and, as such, is a good way in to real partnership with parents. We try to create an environment where children, parents and teachers can be relaxed, confident and secure with each other. This calls for bold initiatives, big hearts, physical and emotional resilience, deep respect for people and children as individuals, and an ability to work hard. The situation is by no means perfect. We are fighting a never-ending battle to indoctrinate new parents, encourage reluctant ones and to support the weaker ones. Discussions are now taking place to expand home involvement for those parents and children who require stretching.

What is certain is the dedication and determination of staff to have parents fully involved in all matters pertaining to our school.

III PRACTICE IN A NURSERY CLASS: SHARING THE BEGINNINGS

Angela Jefferis

Nine months ago I was asked if I would introduce PACT to the nursery where I teach and monitor the results. I agreed, with reservations: it seemed a worthwhile proposition although it would mean extra work in a normally busy day.

The first thing that struck me was that I did not know how many parents already read regularly with their children. This information would obviously help me to decide how to go about starting the scheme. To find out, I conducted a survey of my own. This was done through my usual discussions with the twenty-five parents, all of whom bring their children to school. I found the results very interesting to me as the children's teacher. Only three admitted to never reading with their children, mainly because they 'didn't have the time'. Thirteen said they sometimes read, perhaps two or three times a week, and nine read to their children once or twice a day. One parent's comment was: 'She makes my life a misery. She keeps on and on until I read to her!'

After the survey I held a meeting in the nursery for the parents, at which the headteacher spoke about the importance of parents reading to their children. All but three children were represented by one or other of their parents. It was stressed that it is never too early to read stories to your children, even if they are still 'babes in arms'. Many parents felt that it wasn't necessary to read stories until their child was able to converse fairly fluently and could, therefore, make some comment on whether they liked or disliked a story. By the end of the meeting the parents appeared to understand that, by reading to their children, they not only entertained them but were also preparing the ground for the 'learning to read' process.

The scheme has started well. I have to ensure that there is a varied selection of books for the children to choose from. I have about sixty books for my twenty-five children, ranging from very simple picture books to more detailed stories. I have also had to devise an efficient system of recording the books on loan. The system that I have found works best is to number each book and to have my own list of books with a corresponding number. I have another list with each child's name on it, and as the children choose a book I simply have to write the number next to their name and cross it off as the books are returned. However, I do write the full title of each book on the parents' comment card as a number would be meaningless, especially if they mislaid the book.

Initially the children chose a book twice a week, but I soon discovered that they preferred to keep the book a full week as it gives the parents the opportunity to read it several times to them. 'Likes listening to the story read over and over again. She can tell the story by looking at the facing pictures' was one parent's comment. It is well known that young children appreciate familiar stories.

One of the drawbacks is the wear and tear on the books. However careful the children are, accidents do occur. For example, a younger sibling or dog has torn the book, or, what is not always immediately apparent, the books have been scribbled on inside. However, the parents are generally willing to replace the damaged book, or at least make a contribution. I do believe that the books on loan should be in good condition to start with otherwise the children will not see the point of caring for the ones they borrow. They certainly appear to be horrified when I show them a book which has obviously been misused.

On the whole, the children make their own choice and they enjoy their weekly selection. All the books are displayed on a table and a group of three or four children at a time make their choice. Some take a while and need guidance, particularly the children whose mother tongue is not English, while others have already decided upon their choice in advance. Occasionally they are influenced by their parents, e.g. 'My mum doesn't like Mr Men books', or 'My mum wants me to take a big book'. I have had children choosing the same book two or three times consecutively. This is particularly so with the non-English speaking children. One parent commented: 'He didn't want to let this one go back.'

With each book I send home a card with the child's name, the title of the book, the date and a space for the parent's comment. This has proved to be a very valuable exercise as I have learnt a great deal from their comments. It indicates the more popular books and those thought to be unsuitable for various reasons. The following comments are typical:

The Little Red Hen 'U. enjoyed looking at the pictures while the story was being read to her. I showed her what was happening and she enjoyed seeing the names of the animals. I liked the book because it was easy to understand for a child of U.'s age.'

Mr Impossible 'I liked this one and so did S. It certainly stimulated her imagination – she's going to practise to become invisible.'

Mr Clumsy 'She liked this story, it reminded her of her Dad!'

Our Home 'L. made up her own names for the people in this book, she seemed to enjoy it more.'

Mr Wrong 'He didn't seem to understand the story, so he was unable to appreciate the end.' 'S. liked the changeover at the end and the idea that Mr Wrong could now help Mr Right.'

Topsy and Tim at the Fairground   'She loved this story because she loves funfairs. She knew everything in the book!'

Mouse looks for a House   'M. can read some of this book on his own and enjoys the rest being read to him. Could he have another book similar to this one, please?' 'He was aggravated by this book. I think he was waiting for the story to start.'

Sam and the Firefly   'It was great fun reading the book. L. was in fits of laughter.' 'He was very absorbed in the story.' 'Didn't enjoy it much. Didn't understand it properly.'

Good Night Owl   'Thought it was very funny.' 'L. didn't seem to like this book much. As I was reading it to her she got up and walked away. She found it boring.' 'She likes this book but did not ask to read it very often.' 'Felt very sorry for poor Owl. Loved the bit where he got revenge.'

Although most parents are willing to make some kind of comment, they do need constant encouragement, otherwise they just leave a blank space, or simply write: 'Liked the book'. However, I feel any comment is valuable and an indication of parental support. I try to convey to parents how helpful their comments are, even if they feel rather negative towards a book: 'I think the words of this book are too difficult for R. to understand.' 'She liked the bit where the letter was browning nicely. I must say, I'm fed up with R.H., but she still likes his stuff as much as ever.' 'I found the story boring – but then it wasn't written for me!' You also get delightful comments where a parent has obviously become totally involved in a book: 'T. found the duck's adventures very amusing, considering I had to do the animal imitations.'

PACT is an ongoing concern. We hope that parents will continue to be interested, and feel encouraged enough to involve themselves more in reading with their children, joining the local library, and perhaps making their own books, so that the children can listen to, and learn to read, their parents' and their own language.

IV   PRACTICE IN A SECONDARY SCHOOL: READING
TOGETHER – A COMPREHENSIVE SCHOOL'S
EXPERIENCE

Phil Gryce

The school is situated within a settled south London working-class district. Many of the adult population work locally, in a decaying industrial area; others remain unemployed. A desire for a 'good education' for the children is not reflected in books available at home, or in the use of other cultural resources in the neighbourhood. By the primary-secondary transfer period children have a restricted cultural landscape, strongly tied to the family but loosely linked with the larger world.

The English department of this four-form entry boys' county comprehensive school is a vigorous one, willing to explore new approaches, well resourced with materials, united around key issues. Staff have tended to develop imaginative writing – out of lived experience or sparked by texts newly read – to activate pupils' participation, as a springboard for extending literacy. In-house magazines of pupils' work are published; classrooms are decorated with writings, illustrations, interpretations; a bookshop is opened regularly.

Yet there remained among teachers a nagging concern, echoed elsewhere in the school, for the disproportionate number of low attaining pupils. There was, and is still, a bias in the intake population: few 'high-fliers', many barely functioning readers. The small remedial department could only attend to a few of these latter.

In 1982 this concern led to the temporary provision of a scale post within the English department, with responsibility for 'slow learners'. The brief was open enough to enable the holder to create any fresh opportunity for pupils that seemed suitable. Early in the school year 1982–3 discussion centred round PACT – parental involvement in reading, prompted by an advisory teacher's collection of research findings and school experiences elsewhere. After sounding out colleagues it was decided to initiate a home reading scheme.

Early decisions

1 To introduce a scheme into half the first year – this would give some opportunity to compare progress at the end of a period with 'control' classes; it would also act as a sieve for problems and mistakes, before full implementation.

2 To involve both the English teachers and the pastoral tutors in the scheme:

So that reading was not perceived solely as an 'English' activity.

To utilize existing parent-tutor contacts, modifying the model of parents as passive receivers and of teachers as conveyors of information, bringers of disciplinary 'bad news', towards a more interactive, positive model.

To provide a positive base for contacts between tutors and pupils.

To emphasize the use of pastoral time as a further learning resource, as a chance for an exchange of views.

3 To describe the scheme to parents at the next parents' evening in the school calendar (thoughts of a captive audience?).

4 To build up a bank of books for each class, in addition to those provided by the department and the library.

The head agreed at once that this was a new policy, additional to the annual budget of the department, and should be financed separately as a whole school enterprise.

The librarian, remedial department and other English staff were invited to recommend books for the scheme; much use was made of ILEA's English Centre book box lists; temporary loans were available through ILEA's central loan resources.

The book bank would not at first contain second-language material; it was felt that reading in a mother tongue was to be encouraged but it would be better for the parents to explore their own literature with their children, rather than impose the school's preconceptions; contact addresses of ethnic bookshops and classes were prepared.

The function of the book bank was to encourage easy selection, ready access by pupils, and to foster an atmosphere of relaxed enjoyment of reading; the less able were recognized as reluctant library users.

5   To prepare an attractive leaflet for parents and invite their involvement in a simple recording system.

The booklet

This school has a high reprographics standard. The 'leaflet' rapidly became a booklet, wire-bound, with semi-stiff covers, illustrated with copyright-free professional graphics and cartoons drawn by a pupil. Moral: if parents are valued by the school, then give value to what parents receive by ensuring it looks good. An early choice of illustration was of a teacher figure, extending a grateful hand, smiling broadly, but with an axe hidden behind his back. 'Read or else' seemed to be the message! Subsequent versions blanked out the axe.

The booklet offered a brief rationale for the scheme, and some plain advice:

> When you listen to your child read please:
>> Praise your child.
>> Never get cross.
>> Let him guess or predict new words.
>> If he doesn't recognize a word quickly then tell him it and move on immediately.
>> If he fails to understand lots of words then either stop or read the rest of the book to him yourself.
>> Remember that we want your child to *enjoy* reading.

Contact routes were given: the record card, names of staff, school telephone number. A motif was chosen – a comic trumpeter-herald; this appeared on the front cover, the record card and in the classroom: a readily identifiable figure.

The record

Communication between parents and school was to be by way of a 'book-mark'; this identified the particular week, number of pages read, title of book and space for parent's signature. Overleaf there was room for 'comments'. The book-mark was to be taken with the chosen book and returned at weekly intervals, when a fresh card would be issued.

Staff involvement

Participating teachers took part in briefing sessions, attended by others as well: the remedial department, the senior teacher (pastoral), the head. There was discussion as to back-up support for pupils and parents who were not drawn into the scheme:

The remedial teachers and tutors would try more direct approaches.

The educational welfare officer would be familiarized with the scheme so that she might raise the issue during a home visit, if conditions permitted.

Sixth-form volunteers might be used as 'foster-readers'.

This group agreed what was acceptable reading matter. Only comics were excluded: there was a feeling that the readability of comics was over-estimated, and that parents might consider them 'uneducational'. However, newspapers, magazines and other such materials were all grist to the same mill.

Before the parents' evening

Pupils were introduced to the scheme on the days before the meeting. Books were made available at once and selection was invited, so that as soon as the parents were told, every pupil could bring home a chosen book. Had a weekend intervened without a start being made, some interest would have waned.

The parents' evening

The school had chosen to make its presentation at a meeting, previously announced, for parents to talk with teachers concerning their child's progress. A specially written letter went to the parents of the two classes in the scheme, who were invited to attend somewhat earlier.

The head made the briefest of introductions (but his presence underlined the public value being placed on the venture). A domestic scene was acted out by older pupils, an amusing sketch of how *not* to help a child read at home: mum fussed with the ironing, dad was glued to the football results, the radio was blaring. . . . The organizing teacher talked succinctly and enthusiastically, explained the booklet, introduced the staff involved, allowed time for questions and left the last word to another enactment: a sketch of how *best* to help a child.

During the rest of the evening, the tutors broached the subject again on an individual level, allowing time to discuss related questions: the pressure of other children, making the occasion regular. Reactions were agreeable, with parents anxious to help in some way and glad of an agreed purpose.

There was a display: PACT items, specimen books, a placard for the school library ('What about a Christmas present?'), local library membership cards, adult literacy class notices.

The scheme running

A high rate of participation, 90 per cent plus, was achieved very quickly. Parents who had not attended the meeting were contacted personally by tutors; pupils whose parents had not responded were asked privately if they could approach their parents, and invite them in.

Purchases at the school bookshop increased.

The comments space on the book-marks led to a variety of communications:

'This book is exciting and sad.'
'Very good book and a bit strange.'
'He had an upset tummy, so stayed in bed for the day and he read the book you gave him right through, hope you don't mind.'
'May I suggest he has a different book on Wednesday, as he

heard the story and saw the film on television. This could be the reason for his lack of interest.'

'Gave up *Raiders of the Lost Ark*, could not get into it, so on *Cars and Trucks*.'

'J. is reading a lot better now.'

'Excellent, second best story I've ever read.'

The great majority were more than content with fiction; early fears that some children would not move beyond factual material were allayed. The daily rate of reading was higher than suggested in the booklet – without resulting in any undue strain in the family. The parents used the comments space for sharp observations, questions ('Does he have to read aloud if he's embarrassed?'), excuses for absence, requests for more things to do at home, criticism, praise. A new channel of communication had opened up beyond the scheme; the interaction over a mutually agreed venture led to a more positive seeking of contacts.

Teachers freely responded by using the comments space themselves:

'Is he stretching himself enough?'

'R. has been reading the horror stories for some time now. Are they very frightening? Please change the book if you wish.'

'Glad to see Mark dropped the book he was not enjoying. That's the way!'

'Thanks for the note about S.'s upset . . .'

'Happy New Year!'

In general it was a relaxed interaction, with anxieties readily relieved and mutual encouragement offered.

Record-keeping

Apart from the class teacher keeping the book-marks, an effort was made for pupils to record their own reading. A classroom chart was prepared, as a record of recommendations rather than as a competitive display. Pupils placed beside their name a strip of gummed paper bearing the title of the book read. Colour signified their grading of each book:

> green: highly recommended; very exciting
> blue: nothing special; average
> yellow: awful; unreadable.

What was striking was the rarity of yellow strips. This may have been a reflection of how carefully the book banks were selected, but more likely it reflects pupils' often under-estimated ability to make appropriate selections for themselves (whether by cover, publisher's blurb or reputation).

Measures of success

Within a term the other half of the year joined the scheme. Parents and pupils of the classes 'left out' had expressed keen interest. Staff sensed the scheme was going well and saw no reason to wait for 'results'. The school analyses the London Reading Test scores for the new intake, and a norm-referenced comprehension test is also applied on first entry to the school; but, since the re-test for monitoring purposes is not carried out until the spring term of the pupils' third year, no appropriate use could be made of these scores for assessing the scheme; and there was no wish to add another round of testing. Even without formal measures, staff were confident of the success of the venture.

Indicators of success included:

> more books read by pupils, regardless of attainment;
> improved contacts between parents, pupils and staff;
> a greater enthusiasm and freedom of expression in the classroom when talking about books; there was no need to 'force' discussion, reactions were spontaneous.

Word-of-mouth success

By way of a footnote to the staff's own feeling about the scheme's success, I overheard a conversation at a local primary school, at which secondary school heads were drumming up first-choice support for next year's intake. A group of mothers were trading experiences: the usual horror stories, except for a clear reference to the 'Reading Together' scheme (at that time, this was the only school in the area with such a scheme; in this current year half of the local secondary schools will either have full versions or be launching trials). One mother said:

> The one my son goes to really takes care of him. He has to bring home a book regular and read it to me or his dad; the teacher's always dropping us a line about it, and how good he's doing. If they took girls, I'd be putting my Sally down for it.

8

Does it work?

Readers can hardly have failed to notice that the writers of this book are committed to the idea of PACT, and believe that it can be of the greatest benefit to children's education. But it is time to look at the evidence that this is really so; and this calls for a sober examination of what is actually happening.

It is certainly true that large numbers of teachers are now using the kind of structured scheme advocated in this book, and the great majority claim that children benefit. They speak of improved reading ages, more books read by children, better parent-teacher relationships, the disappearance of mild behavioural problems in the classroom and improved motivation towards reading. These teachers are not necessarily interested in formal evaluation, since they have tasted the fruits of successful parental involvement for themselves, and are already convinced of its value. For them, practice is more convincing than abstract research figures.

And indeed the research, though impressive, does have its limitations. It is notoriously difficult to conduct well-controlled research in the classroom, and the rigorous academic would say that even the highly acclaimed Haringey Project has a number of limitations. For instance, there is no experimental condition in which some of the children in one class received parental help while others in the same class did not. Such a condition would have allowed the researchers to take into account the personal qualities and professional expertise of an individual teacher. However, it would have been ethically unacceptable, to both teachers and parents, to include such a condition. Again, Jenny Hewison and Jack Tizard[6] clearly demonstrated, in a working-class area, that up to 50 per cent of parents already hear their children read on a regular basis which would mean that, even in the control groups, many children would have been heard reading at home. Thus these control groups could not strictly be compared with experimental groups where parents were being asked to hear their children read. For these kinds of reasons it is difficult to claim with certainty that it was the fact of parents hearing their children read at home which caused the improvement in reading standards in the Haringey Project. (See references 2 and 7 for fuller discussion.)

It is also difficult to show that it is the reading activity itself which produces the results. In an extremely interesting set of experiments in Somerset, in which children with reading problems received no special extra help, but had someone to talk with for a short while on a once-a-week basis, Denis Lawrence was able to demonstrate noticeable reading improvement.[17,18] He argued that reading was a skill highly valued by adults, and children who fail to make progress in reading see themselves to be failing as people. Lawrence believed that if the self-image of these children could be improved, then ultimately their reading might improve also. To enhance their self-image, Lawrence arranged for children to be 'counselled', using an approach which allowed them to talk freely and express their personalities in the company of a sympathetic adult. The 'counsellors' were untrained people who were briefed to interact with the child to replicate an ordinary parent-child relationship. This systematic individual counselling did appear to improve reading, as well as self-image. In fact, the children's reading was improved more by following this approach than by being given straight remedial teaching.

Certainly there are limitations to this 'counselling' approach. It has been pointed out that children who can be described as tough-minded or lacking in empathy, and who have a low general anxiety level, do not receive much benefit from such counselling.[19] Nevertheless, the fact that many children do benefit may be one of the keys to understanding why parental help with reading works. It is likely that parents who take the trouble to sit down and work with their child are improving that child's self-image, building up self-confidence and strengthening motivation. Parents can capitalize on the significant relationship they have with their own child, especially where they are secure in the knowledge that they are doing the 'right thing' when collaborating with teachers. Equally important, perhaps, is that parent-teacher collaboration itself – we certainly believe so.

It is clear that statistical investigation into exactly why, and in what ways, children benefit would have to take into account so many widely differing factors as to be quite impossibly complex. That children do benefit is beyond doubt. Whatever the reasons for this, parents, teachers and children extol the merits of parental help with reading; and schools have tried to produce objective as well as anecdotal evidence to back up their faith in its virtues.

Some schools trying to look objectively at their work with parents have analysed reading ages, and a variety of tests have been used. One inner-city junior school demonstrated a 62 per cent improvement in the number of children reading above their chronological age, with many fewer children failing in reading than previously. In fact, reading standards over an

18-month period had shifted upwards dramatically. The school
had hoped to establish an average increase in reading age, but
so many children were scoring above the ceiling of the test (i.e.
above a reading age of 13½/14 years) that this was impossible! It
is not unusual for schools with carefully structured schemes to
find striking overall effects like these produced over an 18–24
month period. Schools report that some individual children
make extraordinary progress over a few months, particularly
those with reading difficulties. For these children, parental help
somehow makes sense of the reading process.

Higher reading ages may make teachers feel better and keep
their political and administrative bosses happy, but they are not
the only measure of what reading is about, nor can they tell us
how the rest of the curriculum is affected. Indeed, it is very
difficult to find objective measures of such intangible things as
improved understanding, motivation and attitude changes, or
overall school or class change. But there are measures which
can act as pointers to such changes.

It can be argued, for instance, that if children were more
strongly motivated to read, and reading standards were improving, then the school would probably need to spend money
on extra books. Success in reading should spur children to read
more, and as reading improves, books at more advanced levels
will be required. So if we ask schools whether they are spending
more money on books, and what sort of books they are buying,
we have an objective measure, which probably reflects the
attitudinal and motivational changes in the school. We sent a
questionnaire to a number of primary schools, asking whether
the introduction of a PACT reading scheme had, over a period
of time, led to their buying more books, and particularly more
advanced books. Schools did indeed report this to be the case.
This even had some unfortunate side-effects, in that for a year or
so schools had to accomplish a difficult balancing act, trying to
ensure that they had some money left over to buy equipment
other than books!

Similarly, we can look at the number of books read by an
individual child. Some schools have been able to demonstrate

that children are reading up to three times as many books after a PACT scheme has been introduced. Children would never produce such an increase in reading activity if they were not enjoying it. So the figures do suggest changes in attitudes toward reading.

Implied changes can also be suggested by asking children how many people hear them read. Some infant schools have done this, and because of their close contact with parents have been able to check the accuracy of the information. The children's answers suggest that home reading is rarely restricted to parents alone. Older brothers and sisters, grandparents and neighbours are often roped in by the child, and the willingness to be so involved suggests positive attitudes about reading in the whole family. The information the schools are collecting has been displayed in attractive chart form to encourage parents, relatives and neighbours to continue their involvement.

Another indicator could be children's attendance, which might possibly be expected to improve where a PACT scheme is operating. Attendance has always been a particular problem for inner-city schools. It is difficult to look at this area because, over the period of eighteen months to two years found necessary to see significant changes in reading, a school may take other initiatives, including 'blitzes' on attendance. In the two junior schools where we obtained attendance figures we found an improvement of a little over 2 per cent. This change, though small, is certainly in the right direction; and a closer analysis of the figures suggested that a small number of children who read at home were now attending steadily, where previously they had frequently missed school.

But it is the anecdotal evidence of numerous individual teachers and headteachers that most clearly demonstrates the effects of home reading schemes. Headteachers have commented on the effect of PACT on their schools:

'Parental involvement in reading in my junior school over the last year is equivalent to an input from six extra teachers!'

'Over the years I have worried that children I send to the juniors from my infant school have not been reading well. After one year of a "parental involvement in reading" scheme I am sending a group of infants whose average reading age is above the national average.'

'The number of children throughout my junior school whose reading age is in excess of their chronological age has risen from under 40 per cent to over 60 per cent and is still rising.'

And class teachers report that individual children become better motivated towards reading, and that they and the children are able to use this motivation to provide a richer reading environment. Many say that PACT schemes improve liaison with parents to such a degree that previous problems are now easily soluble with parental help and insight. Teachers find that parents are much more willing to become involved in class and school activities, from sewing and woodwork to reading and mathematics, and that they develop a fuller awareness of what the teacher is trying to do in the classroom.

'Within two weeks Angela's attitude has changed towards reading. She is now ready and willing to look at books with me.'

'I find it so easy to talk to Mrs Brown now that we have something positive in common – before I seemed to be always complaining about Nicky's behaviour.'

'From what I can make out Mark has his mother, father, grandfather, older sister and his neighbour reading with him most of the time.'

'I must say my class has calmed down considerably over the last month or so since I got the scheme going.'

Teachers committed to a PACT scheme will nearly always say 'It's a lot of hard work', then quickly add 'But it's worth it'. These two reactions were brought home to us when we surveyed thirty-four junior and infant schools, using a short questionnaire. We asked teachers about the difficulties and the advantages when a PACT scheme was introduced into their school. When we analysed the questionnaires, we found a total of thirty-three different comments which reflected some kind of concern. Eighteen of these comments revolved around the pressures on teachers' time, either in the involving of parents or in the day-to-day administration of schemes. Ten mentioned financial pressures in buying new books and replacing old ones (after all, greater use means that books wear out more quickly). Balanced against this, a total of forty positive comments were made, all of which reflected the keen interest and enthusiasm of parents, teachers and children; and many expressed the schools' pleasure that communication between parents and teachers had improved, as well as children's reading.

Given the weight of comment from teachers and head-teachers, it is fair to conclude that educationists involved in PACT schemes believe that involving parents in learning is an extremely positive move towards educating children.

So teachers are committed. What of parents? Teachers may be working hard and extolling the results of their labours, but we also want to know what parents feel. According to teachers, parents are very enthusiastic, and this view is reinforced by looking at the sheer numbers of parents who become involved. We know of two junior schools where 100 per cent of parents hear their children read; more commonly the figure is somewhere between 91 and 98 per cent. Certainly most of the schools operating a formal scheme have 70 per cent or more of their parents involved. In the Haringey research the schools managed to involve 95 per cent of parents, so it would be expected that these percentages would be high. But what do parents themselves say about formal PACT schemes?

In an attempt to investigate parental attitudes toward a formal scheme, ten families from one inner-city school were interviewed by an independent worker, either at home or in the school. These families were asked how they had heard about the scheme, who read with the child, whether it was enjoyable and worthwhile, and what kind of contact they had with the school. The parents were randomly chosen from two class lists of first-year junior children, and the sample reflected the multi-ethnic working-class population of the school. At the time the scheme had been operating in the school for nearly a year.

The main findings were not unexpected. Every parent interviewed had heard about the school scheme from teachers or their children, and were making an effort to hear their children read at home. It was always the mother who heard the child regularly (at least three times a week), although all the fathers participated. In all but one family others, including older brothers and sisters, grandparents and close family friends, were involved. The parents also said that they had positive regular contact with the school.

These confidential interviews also gave insights into parents' attitudes. When asked whether they enjoyed hearing their child read, all but one parent said 'Yes', but many made the proviso that it was difficult to find the time. The problem of finding a convenient and suitable time is made more difficult for parents with three or more children:

> 'If I'm very busy and I've just come home from work and I've got the dinner to get and the three children need to be heard read, and my husband's out – I don't think I'm in the right mind.'

There was one parent who had five children whom different teachers were hoping would be heard reading! In one way or another most parents had overcome this kind of problem, but schools do need to recognize difficulties of this nature and be ready to listen and advise each family, so that reading does not become an unpleasant chore.

Despite the pressures, parents believed that the help they were giving their children was all worthwhile and effective:

> 'It makes him read more; he practises by himself.'
> 'We recognize the books featured on TV.'
> 'My child has matured as a result of the interest taken in her and her reading, she's much less afraid and more open about her reading.'

'Her spelling has improved, she loves reading.'
'He now spontaneously picks up books to read.'

These, remember, are the words of parents, not teachers.

Any concerns that teachers may have felt about involving parents would have proved unfounded, at least in this school. There is a complete dearth of comment which compares their own child with others, or refers to reading level as an end in itself. Instead we get comments such as:

'The books have good stories.'
'I can see the progress he's made – he really understands what he's reading now.'
'It's more fun now, because I don't push her. . . . I tried to push the older girl and it doesn't work.'

These parents have put the skill of reading into a context which demonstrates an understanding of its wider function. Indeed, many parents said they would like to become further involved in the education of their children:

'I would like to help him more. It's not enough to listen to him read, I would like to do something more.'
'I would like to learn more about the school, so I can help her.'

Nevertheless, practical problems still remain in the relationships between parents and teachers:

'I can't talk to the teacher, she's so young.'
'I find it easy to talk to the teacher, 'cos she's younger than me.'
'If only the teacher was female, I would find it so much easier to talk.'
'I think we ought to have more evening meetings so that teachers can explain the things to us.'
'. . . I would like the teacher to explain it all to me, but I don't like going to meetings.'

It is immediately apparent that not all these problems are easily soluble!

Judging by these interviews, and by the many talks we have ourselves had with parents, we can conclude that parents do indeed enjoy the reading sessions with their children, and believe that both they and the children are gaining much from the experience – this despite the many practical problems. Parents are willing to surmount these problems, because they believe it is in their children's best interests, and they have witnessed for themselves the changes that can take place over a period of time.

And now, what do the recipients and supposed beneficiaries of all this collaborative effort feel? If children dislike an idea they usually find excellent ways of sabotaging it, and we must look at the information supplied by teachers and parents for evidence of this.

One good way of sabotaging a PACT scheme would be regularly to lose books that are taken home. Teachers find that this is not a problem. One school we know did lose a number of books, but when they introduced folders to carry books and record cards in, the problem virtually disappeared. Generally, children willingly take books home and bring them back to school. Teachers report that what concerns children most is that their parents do not always manage to hear them read. In isolated cases, parents fail to hear children read at all, and this can lead to problems for a child which need sensitive handling by the teacher (see chapter 5). Far more often teachers report discussions between themselves and children which revolve around their home reading, often prompted by the child's own excitement:

'My mum thought this book was very funny, we did laugh over . . .'

'Please can I have another book about this gang, mummy and I want to read some more about them.'

'Mr Jones upstairs was very pleased with the way my reading was improving.'

'We never started the book last night, Dad and I spent all the time looking at the boats on the cover.'

> 'Dad and me and my sister read that book called *The Blakely Ghost*. Dad and I really enjoyed it and thought the bit talking about the play itself was interesting but my younger sister skipped over that bit. But Dad and I thought that was OK as she didn't miss out on the main story.' (10-year-old boy)

The obvious enjoyment of these children speaks for itself. It looks as though we can safely conclude that PACT reading schemes do work, and that all the participants – children, parents and teachers – believe it is worthwhile. Perhaps we should finish this chapter with two quotes which succinctly put the views of children:

> 'Dad and I read the *Wall Street Gang* together, he read some and I read some. I think I read better than he does. It was such a good story we read nearly half the book . . . it was such a good book we didn't even switch on the television.' (10-year-old boy)

> 'My mum reads to my two-month-old baby sister, I think she is right 'cos reading is so much fun and you've got to learn it, ain't you?' (8-year-old boy)

9

Some variations on the theme

So far, we have described a model which has proved its worth in numerous schools; but there are other ideas and techniques which should be considered. These can supplement our main model, and perhaps in certain areas replace it. The variations discussed in this chapter are in no way an exhaustive review of all the initiatives that teachers have taken, but they are intended to demonstrate the great variety of forms that involving parents in education can take, many of them fun as well as rewarding. Most will fulfil the main elements we have cited for involving parents successfully, namely, starting a trusting partnership, sharing information and maintaining a dialogue. Where this is not the case, they are often an integral part of a wider school project.

The most obvious variation is to bring parents into the school itself. This practice has a long and honourable tradition, and it is a common sight, especially in nursery and primary schools, to see parents helping out enthusiastically in activities such as school plays, sports, trips, cooking and so on. By involving parents in this kind of wholesale way, the school is able to provide a natural meeting-place. Parents themselves can then develop, possibly with the aid of teachers, many different activities from which their children will eventually gain advantage. For example, in an inner-city school with a large proportion of non-English-speaking parents, teachers and parents have organized English language classes. These classes would never have been viable, in terms of attendance or success, if they had not arisen from groups of parents themselves getting together and discussing the need for them, and how they could successfully operate. Many such parent-teacher initiatives exist, and they nearly always arise from the needs of children, whose parents as a group wish to help them more. Sometimes the initiatives are quite ingenious. In one infant school, a parent who could speak no English participated by painting traditional designs on children's hands. This was a talent she had developed in her own country, and her skills stimulated much discussion between parents, children and teachers as to the origin and meaning of the designs.

It is much less common, but apparently on the increase, to see parents in the classroom actually helping individuals or small groups of children with their work. Unfortunately this is not yet always recognized as acceptable professional practice. Of the headteachers who do allow parents to, say, hear children read, there are still many who keep a wary eye as to clear differentiation between parent and teacher roles. Parents may be given euphemistic titles such as 'parent listeners', and relegated to a small room somewhere in the school. Nevertheless, where this is happening at all it is a major professional step forward, and must enhance children's learning and parent-teacher relationships. No one would advocate that parents should be brought into classrooms on such a scale that rooms would be crowded, or that they should necessarily be present for substantial parts of the day. We do believe, though, that such practice should be considered professionally acceptable, and that the work of parents should be fully acknowledged as beneficial to the children's education. This would mean raising the status of parents in a school, and accepting their role as integral to a child's school life.

A school may wish to do more than involve its own parents in reading, either at home or in school. It may want to take its message into every household, and so make the whole community aware of the importance of reading, and of how children can be helped. As a first step the school could provide a well-run bookshop which would bring interesting, readable books to the attention of parents. To affect the community as a whole, larger projects need to be considered.

One school, which already had a bookshop run by parents and teachers, decided to run a bookstall in a local market for just one day, in a joint project with a local library. After gaining permission from the local borough council and the market inspector, they erected a stall alongside the more usual food, clothing and oddments stalls found in a street market. The main aim of the exercise was not to sell books, but to disseminate information. Passers-by were stopped and told about the importance of reading with children. Information was available about the school, local libraries and bookshops, and relevant local associations, together with a short pamphlet on how children could be helped with their reading. Every person stopped was also given a lapel sticker with the inscription 'Read with your child'. This had a dual function, in that it not only reminded people of the conversation they had had with stall-holders, but also publicized the school's beliefs. Incidentally, it further ensured that the same people were not waylaid again when subsequently passing the stall.

Of the hundreds of people stopped by the teachers and parents manning the stall, only three were not prepared to talk and listen once they had satisfied themselves they were not being stopped by a religious or political organization! They were intrigued to find a school stall in the market place, and reacted with positive interest. Many suggested that this was a better place for teachers and parents to meet than on school territory, and that it was right for the local community to know what was happening inside the school. These views were expressed so often that they must reinforce the belief that many parents do feel inferior when visiting the school, and thus are not meeting teachers on equal terms. Meeting parents on their own familiar ground without actually intruding into their homes was probably what enabled a good dialogue to develop between stallholders and shoppers – despite the harassment of being stopped in the first instance!

Not that everybody needed to be stopped. The attractive display of children's books drew a large number of people directly to the stall. Many browsed through the books for some time, and talked with the stallholders about which books would be suitable for their children, and where they could go to find more.

From this kind of exercise schools will make little or no financial profit, as they can normally buy books only at retail price; but it does mean that a wide variety of people can see which books teachers believe should be read. Such knowledge can be useful for Christmas or birthday presents, and could indirectly influence for the better the range of reading materials held by corner shops and newsagents. There is no reason why the market stall idea could not be extended into other places frequented by local people, such as large stores, supermarkets and building societies.

One good example of using public places was the campaign launched by the Ladywood Early Language Project team, led by Joy Workman. The team wanted to publicize the notion that young children's language could be enriched if parents spent more time talking to them. To do this they gave out badges inscribed with the slogan 'Mum, talk to me . . .' to all the customers of a well-known supermarket, and had a display inside the store. The response from parents was enormous and gave the project team a number of good starting-points for further work with parents. Stores have also accepted displays of children's work from schools, and if asked may be persuaded to do even more; after all, why should a store turn down an idea which keeps shoppers on its premises a little longer to be parted from their money?

The market stall idea does require a considerable amount of work from the school, but only over a relatively short period of time. The talking-points it creates, and the teacher-parent contact it provides, remain long after the stall has been taken down. The novelty value of such an exercise in itself brings parents, children and teachers together, particularly if children can be involved in designing and producing posters and materials for the stall.

Using novelty value as a means of taking education into the community is a stratagem that has no bounds, and schools have set many precedents. It is now common for schools to be represented at local shows, usually with a display of children's work; and, with a little thought, such events could be a real source of parent-teacher-child contact. Parents always like to see children's work on display, particularly their own children's; but how much richer this experience would be if teachers were available for an informal conversation. And it is not only their children's work that parents like to see displayed – they also enjoy seeing the children themselves on display, and letting others see them too! Year after year schools have exploited this susceptibility, and entertained hordes of parents with plays, pantomimes and concerts performed by children. This has been taken further by schools who enter local public events such as carnivals. One school we know chose 'book characters' as their theme for a local carnival float. Some children were on the float, many were dressed up by parents to follow it, and many more were handing out leaflets and reading-slogans. Parents, children and teachers alike derived a lot of fun from this; but at the same time the school managed to get its message about reading across to parents and children, and to revitalize a PACT scheme which had started to falter after about eighteen months.

So far, we have concentrated on projects carried out by individual schools, all of which have created a considerable amount of work for teachers. The most effective means of reducing a workload is to share the work with others, which is one of the reasons why a whole-school approach had been adopted throughout this book. However, there is no reason why the act of sharing should not go further than the gates of one school, and include other schools and agencies. One such project was a week long 'Book-in' organized by a group of ten primary schools in fairly close proximity to each other, in liaison with local borough libraries.

The aims of this event were to heighten the awareness that books are fun among children and parents, to help maintain the involvement of parents in the children's reading, and to provide food for thought about books and their uses. Each school was expected to organize a small number of events for itself, some of which could be shared by other schools. The local library also organized two events a day, the content sometimes duplicated, to which schools could bring children and parents. Luckily the library had a hall which could easily accommodate 150 people when necessary. One member of staff represented each school on a planning and co-ordinating committee, together with the local librarians. The committee organized a very wide range of activities, including:

Presentation of plays written by groups of children.
Fancy-dress shows based on book characters.
Coffee mornings.
A display of children's art with a book theme at the local library.
School and class story-reading sessions.
Visiting story-tellers, who included inspectors and children's authors.
Children's entertainments such as Punch and Judy.
Plays by theatrical groups.
Films of books.
Displays of books.
School bookshops run by children and parents and kept open all week.

Special displays of children's work in the school.

Stories presented in a variety of ways to other children in the school.

The results of this ten-school 'Book-in' can best be gauged by its effect on the children. Their work output before, during and after the week-long programme increased, and a general interest and excitement about reading and books was aroused. Schools reported that parental interest had been substantial, and all agreed that the effects had been very beneficial to the children.

Sometimes schools are anxious to ensure that particular groups of children get all the help they need. One such group are those children whose families' first language is not English. Believing it to be important that these children should experience their own home culture in their education, some schools have persuaded parents to write 'books' about their lives in their country of origin. This is not usually an easy task in the first instance, but once some examples are available, many parents agree to become authors. One school in particular devised a successful strategy which is worth giving in some detail.

The school first compiled an explanatory leaflet on 'How to become a school author' which, as simply as possible, suggested to parents that the school wanted them to write a short account of their childhood daily life. The leaflet also described how the school would assist them. A group of ethnic-minority parents then received a letter inviting them to a meeting to discuss the project, and at this meeting the leaflet was shown and discussed. The teacher organizing the event telephoned the parents two weeks later, asking them whether they were interested in participating (telephoning gets a more direct response than writing!). A visit was made to the home of those parents who agreed to the idea, to decide on the format of their book; at this stage, too, decisions were made about the length of the book and who would illustrate it. Usually, illustrations were produced by the parents' own children. Once a parent had produced the text and illustrations, the school took responsibility for typing up the story, laying out the book and producing a final product of good quality. Copies of the books were given to the writers and their children, and many went into classrooms throughout the school. Some books went to other schools and quite a number were sold in local book-shops, which helped to finance the project.

This kind of activity demonstrates the school's belief in the importance of the home culture and brings parents into the learning process in an area where they would probably have more to offer than the teacher. The more 'professional' the format of the final product, the more weight it will carry, and the more parents will want to participate. Also, if the book is used in contexts other than within the school, other parents become interested and are encouraged to participate, by which time the existing parent authors can take some of the burden from the teacher. Obviously activities such as this should not be considered in isolation, but should be part of a wider drive to build a bridge between home and school for children of different ethnic origins. And there is, of course, every reason why such a project should be used with indigenous children and parents as well.[20] It stimulates much family and school discussion, as well as providing the school with a continual flow of interesting books.

Book-writing is a powerful way of involving parents, but it is difficult to do on a large scale unless a school and its staff are prepared to turn themselves into a publishing concern and printing works! An easier way of involving parents whose first language is not English is to invite them to participate in a special project such as that run by one secondary school. A first-year class studied world folk tales and invited parents, among others, to tell traditional stories and to talk about their youth, language and customs. The children were asked to produce taped and written versions of stories, with help from parents and sixth formers. Some extremely good work was produced by the children. One difficulty with such a project is that it relies on parents feeling competent and confident about participating. For this reason it works best if teachers and parents are already collaborating and are able to support each other.

We could not finish this chapter without giving special consideration to those children who have reading difficulties. 'Paired reading', as a technique to aid such children, is now being used in a large number of primary schools as well as some secondary schools. This technique is not new, but its usefulness for individual children was refined by Morgan and Lyons in 1979[21] and its efficacy on a wider scale demonstrated in various projects in London, Derbyshire and elsewhere. Essentially the technique consists in 'simultaneous' reading, in which the child and parent read aloud together, and 'independent' reading, in which the child takes over and reads himself when he feels confident enough to do so. The parent praises the child frequently, and only joins in again when the child hesitates for long over a word. (For a more detailed description see references 21–3.)

This technique works very well; reading gains both in accuracy and comprehension for many children, and children's improved attitudes toward reading, school and their work generally have impressed teachers. But parents do need considerable support and training because the instructions and rules are very detailed. To this end, home visits can be made, or regular meetings held at the school. A school can reasonably supervise the parents of a limited number of children at a time, but the technique is really only appropriate for those children with some degree of reading difficulty – children who read well could even be inhibited by so structured an approach. In our view, paired reading cannot have a very wide application because of the intensive work involved; the more general approach advocated in this book demands less work from teachers and has been shown to help children with reading difficulties. Paired reading is, however, a very useful tool to use within a well-co-ordinated PACT scheme, and can supplement the school's armoury for working with those parents whose children have persistent difficulties.

Paired reading is not the only technique involving parents that teachers have used in working with children with reading difficulties. One remedial teacher,[24] for example, argued that the structured remedial programmes designed for these children usually consisted in pruning the sight vocabulary to a small number of frequently used words, while at the same time gradually introducing the spelling patterns of the language. This teacher asked parents to take most of the responsibility for teaching the sight vocabulary, while he himself taught the spelling patterns. Parents were given advice and materials to provide and play reading games with their children. This method worked extremely well. It was noticeable, though, that where parents did not attend the supporting reading-workshop session, much less progress was made. This reinforces our view that regular contact between parents and teachers is essential if a PACT scheme is to flourish.

The ideas we have presented are only a small selection from the variety of present practice involving parents in children's learning. We hope they demonstrate that the only restraints on parent-teacher collaboration are the limits of imagination; a formal PACT system, integrated into a school's policy, can lead eventually to parent involvement on a large scale.

As it endeavours to meet the needs and wishes of its own parents, children and teachers, each scheme acquires the stamp of individuality. This ensures that schemes do not become a chore, and a school can project its own personality into the local community feeling that it has something unique to offer. In the variations we have cited, teachers have tried hard to reflect in their work the knowledge and values of their local community and have examined ideas which enable teachers and parents to find common ground to help children with their learning; but there are still many avenues to be explored.

10
Ways forward

Our main theme has been the way in which an open, trusting partnership between parents and teachers can be generated. We have expressed our belief that parents and teachers must first meet to start this partnership, that they need to share their respective knowledge, and that reliable structures must be established to maintain the new dialogue. We have used reading as an initial focus, and it is clear that schools have been able to operate structured reading schemes with considerable success. Perhaps the main reason for their success is that reading is of prime interest both to teachers and parents, and co-operating in such an important field enables them to work together constructively. We believe, though, that reading is to be regarded as a starting-point, as common ground that is relatively easy to establish, and that we must look for further ways to develop this partnership.

We have no intention of considering the general theme of linking home and school, which is well documented elsewhere,[25, 26] except to note one point. Namely, that a PACT scheme develops a relationship between parent and teacher which, like all good relationships, needs encouragement in order to be sustained and allowed to grow. Many teachers have commented on improved parent-teacher relationships with the introduction of PACT and they realize how important it is to listen to what parents have to say. Such listening, on both sides, can help develop the relationship. If this is accepted and acted upon, the dialogue between every school and its parents can develop in a variety of different ways, the richness of which we can only speculate on.

Some schools have attempted to develop their partnership by involving parents in other aspects of the curriculum: numeracy and primary science have been common choices, often because parents wanted to know more about these areas. Metrication and set theory have muddled many of us, but where schools have discussed these topics with parents the response has been positive and many have expressed their gratitude for the demystification. Such knowledge enables parents to be more responsible for their children's learning; they need and want to be informed if they are to exert their parental rights and responsibilities in the best interests of their children. Parents have the right to be given information, and teachers are in a position to facilitate this.

Teachers have a large body of knowledge, gained through their training and their experience, which would help most parents. Their familiarity with this knowledge may sometimes cause teachers to regard it as common sense, but it is also true that there is little sense common to all. Let us look at some examples where information can be shared with parents to the benefit of their children.

Nearly everyone knows the location of local libraries, and is aware of the fact that these institutions lend out books, which if not brought back can lead to fines! What is not always so well known is the amount and kind of knowledge the library carries about the local environment. It can be a mine of information about local history, geography and events, on future planning within the locality, on how to make contact with professionals, how to gain further educational qualifications and on recreational activities. There are many examples of librarians going into schools to talk to children, parents and teachers about libraries and their resources, and perhaps this should become more commonplace. But it is possible to make libraries still more of a community focus if schools and local librarians organize joint events, and encourage parents and children into the library to make good use of the resources. It is the fact that the school acknowledges the educational importance of libraries and actively supports them that will help maximize their use by parents and children.

Some local libraries have schemes which are of great interest to schools. One such scheme in the south-east is the 'Family book evening',[27] in which children and parents are invited to the library about twice a term to discuss books. Many children's fiction books are made specially available, and children are allowed to take home as many as they wish. They tell the others about one of them at the next session, and the librarians also talk about books they have recently read. Parents too are asked to read the occasional book and discuss it in the group. This scheme has been very successful in attracting large numbers of children, but the amount of parental participation has not been overwhelming. If local schools had taken more of an initiative to encourage parents, as well as children, to attend the sessions this might have made all the difference. The evenings were specifically for families, yet as publicity came largely from the schools, parents were not always fully aware of the importance of their attendance, let alone the advantages to the family that might accrue.

Such joint ventures need not generate an unacceptable workload for teachers. It is more the belief that they are worthwhile and the moral support that is given that matter. In any case, once parents and teachers are working as partners it is possible to share the burden of organizing events and activities.

This sharing can itself provide channels by which more information can be imparted to parents: an obvious way is jointly to publish a parents' newspaper or letter. A good example is that produced by the parents and teachers of Belfield School in Rochdale.[3] Such a paper can cover a wide range of information, including items on what families might do at the weekend, which museums and sites are worth a visit, and interesting local events. And there can be articles on helping a child more directly, such as how to make toys with younger children, and how to help your child to spell. Consumer complaints and the function of social services are typical subjects welcomed by parents. There are endless possibilities; papers produced by teachers and parents may one day even challenge the local newspaper!

The whereabouts of new and second-hand bookshops, particularly in inner-city areas, is information that should always be brought to the attention of parents. When parents buy books for their children they often buy those which are readily available in local shops. Unfortunately many such books are poor value for money in educational terms, and the money could be better spent if some guidance were given – a good reason for having a school bookshop. We are not trying to decry the comics or television annuals, alphabet colouring books or puzzle books which are available in the local newsagent. What we do believe is that children should also have ready access to high quality books, not only in schools or borrowed from libraries, but available on their own bookshelf at home and shared by the whole family.

As the partnership develops, the needs and wishes of both parents and teachers become more apparent, and all that is necessary is to find suitable ways of meeting these needs. A number of schools run discussion groups which meet regularly. These enable parents and teachers to get to know each other better and to discuss some topics in depth. Sometimes these discussion groups concentrate solely on matters which directly concern the children, such as how the school liaises with parents and how this could be improved. Outsiders can sometimes help the school to tackle a subject which requires more specialist knowledge. One good example is that of an educational psychologist and a teacher (a husband and wife team) who, jointly with teachers, ran a series of discussions on 'Adolescence' with the parents of a girls' secondary school.[28] Parents warmly appreciated the chance to look closely at a topic that concerned them, in conjunction with professionals who knew their children. Often the topics are broader in nature, and may include discussions on parents' rights or the implications of education acts. Attendance by parents at such meetings is generally high, doubtless because they believe that the knowledge they gain may help their child, but also because they find the subjects discussed interesting and worth knowing about in themselves.

If a good working partnership between parents and teachers can be started when a child first attends school and maintained throughout his school life, then parents and teachers can feel that they have given that child the fullest possible support. Most of what we have said about partnership is applicable to children of all ages. But when the child reaches secondary school, the focus of co-operation may well need to shift. While the formal PACT reading schemes we have discussed in this book have much to offer children in their first year or so at their new school, we recognize that if all secondary teachers and all parents are to maintain a partnership, more will be needed to bring them together.

Parental involvement, as we have noted, is much less commonplace in secondary schools. This is at least partly due to the subject-based curriculum: many parents declare a lack of knowledge in one or more subjects, and certain teachers guard their subject specialisms with some jealousy. One potential focus which should, however, be of interest to all parents and teachers is an awareness of how to enable children to learn. Parents will voice such questions as:

'How do I make sure Mark learns his homework?'
'How should Tracey revise for her exams?'

'How do I know if Terry is making good notes?'
'How can I get Sylvia to organize herself?'

The kinds of skills needed to be able to learn effectively are often called learning skills or study skills, and we think that children's learning could be enhanced if parents had more knowledge of these.

One local authority has produced a booklet for pupils called 'Effective learning skills – a pupil guide' which can be given to pupils and discussed with parents.[29] The booklet covers such ground as how to organize a workload, how to store and re-trieve information, how to prepare and revise for exams, how to cope with stress, and so on. All of this is put in the form of clear and practical advice which removes many parental fears and anxieties about their inability to help secondary-age chil-dren. Instead, parents find themselves in a position to help their child in the evening, not so much, perhaps, with the content of any homework but with how a task can be accomplished successfully. This looks like a promising basis for a partnership between parent and child, with both intent on improving the overall quality of the child's learning.

There are other possible focuses which can be used to bring parents and teachers together in secondary schools. Discussion groups held for parents can explore the actual subjects taught, as well as more general matters, and sometimes parents can be involved directly in their children's homework. Ebbutt and Barber,[30] for example, asked parents to help their first-year children with passages for comprehension covering a range of school subjects, which formed part of a structured programme to help children who had reading difficulties. The children gained in many respects, only one of which was reading com-petence. They gained in confidence, and in their ability to work well in various school subjects. It looks as though this kind of programme helped these children develop better learning skills, which reinforces our belief that secondary school teachers and parents should look closely at this area as a promising focus for future partnership.

The offer of partnership can be extended by schools to other members of the community. We have seen that schools often invite parents to help in a variety of ways, but there is also a tradition whereby schools invite other people into school to share specialist knowledge or experience with children. Such people are not brought in to replace teachers' skills, but to supplement them. Perhaps the commonest reason for bringing in outsiders is to give career guidance, but children of all ages can benefit from contact with specialist skills and enthusiasms. Indeed, many people are prepared to give up their time to do this because they enjoy it, and teachers can capitalize on this goodwill. But there is at least one section of the community to which teachers could look for more substantial assistance: people who have the time and often the willingness to become more closely involved with a school. Such people are the children's grandparents and, more generally, old and retired people. Bringing older people and children together would have a dual function, in that children could get extra help while their helpers would feel involved and useful.

Old people need to take an active role in the community, and if they do not may have feelings of redundancy and uselessness. These people have the benefit of a lifetime of experiences, and many practical and creative skills. In an age when the natural links between old people and children have been eroded by general mobility and the weakening of family ties, perhaps it is important to make a deliberate effort to bring them together. Certainly old people would feel valued; but children would also gain. They would gain from old people's time and energy, from their experience and attitudes, from their wisdom and knowledge.

There are several schemes throughout the country in which old people are involved in school life, as reported by Help the Aged.[31] And Denis Lawrence[32] asked grandparents, among others, to counsel children, which proved very effective. If co-operation with old people is set up and structured as carefully as with parents, teachers may then find they have a resource from the community which is almost as beneficial as involving parents themselves.

Several times during the course of this book the idea of children or parents themselves producing reading material has been mentioned. This is potentially the basis of a considerable educational resource, one that might be extended into the community, and which has as yet been scarcely tapped. It is widely recognized that infant school children learn through reading what they themselves, and their peers, have written, but this recognition is less often applied at other age levels. Yet the principles regarding the prediction and understanding of one's own language and experience are surely the same for all children – and in fact this approach has been shown to work well with many age-groups. The idea has been most fully developed by advocates of 'language experience approaches'.[33,34]

The realization that parents and children might be encouraged to write for themselves, for each other, and for other children, dovetails with the call for extra reading material that PACT schemes tend to create. Schools may find that such writing gives them ready access to plenty of good material – material dealing with the children's own experience, and in language they can understand. It is possible to organize a resource like this on a large scale, and in at least one area such an attempt is being made. The Durham Printing Project[35] accepts children's written work from schools and produces from it attractive, illustrated 'books', for the originating schools and others. The children have become 'real' authors, feeling their work is valued and taken seriously. This idea might be taken up by local authorities and voluntary agencies – and why should the 'books' not have wider audiences than just the schools? The possibilities of sharing experience, and developing children's literacy skills, in this way might include other sections of the community. In one East End borough a local high street shop[36] sells books and publications, numbers of which have been written by people in the area – and it serves at the same time as a coffee shop and meeting place. This is the kind of focal point from which community ventures of all kinds can develop. One such development, we suggest, might consist in an exchange of written material, by which schools supply children's work to the centre and people from the community write for the schools. Such writing might have a particular local flavour – historical, geographical, social, personal (what a resource this would also be for the teacher with responsibility for environmental studies!).

We have tried to look at ideas which will develop parent-teacher partnership, and help to draw on resources from the local community. In view of all the hard work this will entail for teachers, how are they themselves to be supported?

Although practising teachers have shown themselves well able to work with parents, there is still a need to help them refine their skills and develop their knowledge. In-service training in this area should be focused largely on the school itself, to bring out its individuality and its teachers' personal skills; but it is also important to bring teachers together from different schools to share ideas and expertise. One effect of such sharing is the advice schools can give each other where difficulties are being experienced. The tone of this book is manifestly optimistic – but we have sometimes been told of a particular point we have tried to make: 'It's all very well to claim that, but when we tried it. . . .' Where other teachers from other schools are present, though, such a remark is almost sure to be greeted with 'Oh no, we've had no trouble there at all – our difficulty has been . . .' which in turn will be contradicted by a quite different experience from another school. It is clear that particular schools experience different areas of success and failure, and that the various problems are not so much integral to the basic ideas of PACT itself as arising from a school's own character and circumstances. Through sharing their methods for achieving success, schools can help each other to alleviate difficulties far better than can any generalized outsider's treatise – like this book.

Obviously schools can do much for themselves in this way, but it is also the responsibility of the local education authority to provide in-service training and support for parent-teacher schemes. Many schemes in various parts of the country would have foundered if not given at least the moral support of their LEAs. One example is the support the Inner London Education Authority has given to PACT conferences and initiatives. The PACT movement would never have flourished in so many schools but for the Authority's backing. Through such organizations, and their own advisory services, LEAs can enable knowledge, expertise and resources to be shared.

But it is not only in-service training that needs to be considered. Looking to the future, the initial training of teachers should also incorporate a large element on the subject of working with parents. It is true that training colleges find it difficult to timetable the conflicting claims of the various elements which form their courses, but despite this congestion we believe that there is no longer any case for excluding the study of parent-teacher co-operation in children's learning from the central core of knowledge with which teachers start their professional life. When we have talked to teachers in their initial training we have found them excited and inspired by the concept of PACT, and this should be an encouragement to those planning college courses.

Co-operation between parents and teachers in children's learning is a comparatively new field, although the research findings and examples of good practice are accumulating. The one clear direction in which such co-operation does take us is away from the traditional split between home and school and toward a genuine sharing of responsibility for children's education. We believe that this could signal a real turning-point for children and their learning. Most significant of all has been the enthusiasm of everyone involved in the schemes. Underlying any work of this kind is the permanent reservoir of love and concern that parents feel for their children, and perhaps it is for this reason above all that children stand to gain from a close partnership between their parents and their schools. Whatever the future holds, we are now convinced that parents must be included as partners in their children's learning.

Notes and references

1 Centre for Urban Educational Studies (CUES), Robert Montefiore School, Vallance Road, London E1.
2 Tizard, J., Schofield, W. N. and Hewison, J. (1982) 'Collaboration between teachers and parents in assisting children's reading', *British Journal of Educational Psychology*, 52 (I), 1–15.
3 Jackson, A. and Hannon, P. (1981) *The Belfield Reading Project*, Rochdale, Belfield Community Council.
4 Pritchard, D. and Rennie, J. (1978) *Reading: Involving Parents*, Coventry Education Committee, Community Education Project.
5 Wilby, P. (1981) 'The Belfield experiment', *Sunday Times Review*, 29 March 1981.
6 Hewison, J. and Tizard, J. (1980) 'Parental involvement in reading attainment', *British Journal of Educational Psychology*, 50 (3), 209–15.
7 Hewison, J. (1982) 'Parental involvement in the teaching of reading', *Remedial Education*, 17 (4), 156–62.

8 Bullock Report (1975) *A Language for Life*, Report of the Committee of Inquiry appointed by the Secretary of State for Education and Science, London, HMSO.

9 Nicholson, T. (1979) 'What parents know about reading – and what we need to tell them', paper presented at ANZAAS Congress, University of Auckland.

10 Young, M. and McGeeney, P. (1968) *Learning Begins at Home*, London, Routledge & Kegan Paul.

11 Holt, J. (1965) *How Children Fail*, Harmondsworth, Penguin.

12 Hargreaves, D. (1982) *The Challenge for the Comprehensive School: Culture, Curriculum and Community*, London, Routledge & Kegan Paul.

13 Moon, C. and Moon, B. (1973) *Individualized Reading*, University of Reading.

14 Glynn, T. (1980) 'Parent-child interaction in remedial reading at home'. In Clark, M. M. and Glynn, T. (eds) *Reading and Writing for the Child with Difficulties*, University of Birmingham.

15 Beveridge, M. and Jerrams, A. (1981) 'Parental involvement in language development: an evaluation of a school-based parental assistance plan', *British Journal of Educational Psychology*, 51(3) 259–69.

16 Smith, Theresa (1980) *Parents and Preschool*, London, Grant McIntyre.

17 Lawrence, D. (1971) 'The effects of counselling on retarded readers', *Educational Research*, 13 (2), 119–24.

18 Lawrence, D. (1973) *Improved Reading through Counselling*, London, Ward Lock Educational.

19 Lane, D. (1976) 'Limitations of counselling with retarded readers', *Remedial Education*, 2 (3), 120–1.

20 Tizard, B., Mortimore, T. and Burchell, B. (1981) *Involving Parents in Nursery and Infant Schools*, London, Grant McIntyre.

21 Morgan, R. and Lyons, E. (1979) 'Paired reading: a preliminary report on a technique for parental tuition of reading to retarded children', *Journal of Clinical Psychology and Psychiatry*, 20(2), 151–60.

22 Bushell, R., Miller, A. and Robson, D. (1982) 'Parents as remedial teachers', *Association of Educational Psychologists' Journal* 5(9), 7–13.

23 Heath, A. (1981) 'A paired reading programme', ILEA, private communication.

24 Davies, R. (1978) 'A joint parent-teacher programme for the reading instruction of poor and non-readers', *Remedial Education*, 13 (4), 188–92.

25 Craft, M., Raynor, J. and Cohen, L. (1980) *Linking Home and School*, London, Harper & Row.

26 Community Education Development Centre, Briton Road, Coventry. 'Outlines: A Source Pack for Community Education' (1981).

27 Thorpe, D. (1982) 'Family reading groups: the beginnings of a community experience in West Hertfordshire', *Reading*, 16 (3), 143–52.

28 Barnett, R. L. and Barnett, B. R. (1984) 'A series of parent-teacher workshops to discuss adolescent development in young girls: a pilot scheme', unpublished paper, Child Guidance Training Centre.

29 Healy, M. and Goodhand, L. (1983) 'Effective learning skills – a pupil guide', ILEA, Learning Resources Branch.

30 Ebbutt, C. M. and Barber, E. (1979) 'A homework reading scheme for backward readers in a secondary school', *Reading*, 13 (2), 25–31.

31 Help the Aged, Highbury Corner, London N1.

32 Lawrence, D. (1972) 'Counselling of retarded readers by non-professionals', *Educational Research*, 15 (1), 48–54.

33 Cooper, M. G. (1967) 'The Language Experience Approach to Reading', *Reading*, 1 (2), 20–4.

34 Stauffer, R. G. (1980) *The Language Experience Approach to the Teaching of Reading*, New York, Harper & Row.

35 Durham Printing Project, Youth Training Scheme, Durham University School of Education. Director: Jack Gilliland.

36 Centreprise, Kingsland High Street, London E8.

Index